BAKER STUDIES IN BIBLICAL ARCHAEOLOGY

SIR WILLIAM M. RAMSAY

ARCHAEOLOGIST AND
NEW TESTAMENT SCHOLAR

A Survey of His Contribution to
the Study of the New Testament

by
W. Ward Gasque

Foreword by
F. F. Bruce

BAKER BOOK HOUSE
Grand Rapids, Michigan

PHOTOLITHOPRINTED BY CUSHING - MALLOY, INC.
ANN ARBOR, MICHIGAN, UNITED STATES OF AMERICA
1 9 6 7

TO MOTHER,
as a small token of
appreciation for your
sacrifice on my behalf.

CONTENTS

FOREWORD

Although Sir William Ramsay's life and mine overlapped by thirty years, and we belonged to the same university, we never met. Seventeen years before I started my undergraduate career in the University of Aberdeen, he had retired from the Chair of Humanity (Latin) there, and lived for the rest of his life in Edinburgh. Once, in my schoolboy days, I received indirectly a piece of advice from him — that I should beware of dissipating my intellectual energies, as this had been the downfall of many promising young Scots. I have remembered his advice; I am not so sure that I have followed it.

Many of my teachers, at school and university, were pupils of Ramsay, products of the classical discipline inculcated by him and his colleague John Harrower, Professor of Greek. (Harrower was inducted to the Greek Chair in the same year, 1886, as Ramsay became professor of Humanity; but while Ramsay retired in 1911 at the then inordinately early age of sixty, Harrower continued in the Greek Chair for forty-five years in all, until the infirmities of old age compelled him to relinquish it). Of Ramsay and Harrower, two of their distinguished pupils have written:

> No two men could be more unlike; undergraduate rumour had it, many years afterwards, that they were personally unacquainted. Yet, all unconsciously, they made an ideal combination — how effective many of us realized only long afterwards — and between them they built up a school of classical learning which had no equal, outside Oxford and Cambridge, in Britain. Ramsay's contribution to the Aberdeen Classical School was the inspiration of a gifted maker of knowledge; Harrower's was that of a great teacher. What either lacked the other was there to supply. When Ramsay translated *di deaeque omnes* as "all ye inhabitants of heaven, male and female," we felt that it didn't really matter, for we could have told him, as Grecians, how those things were done. When Harrower, for he too was human, began to make Pericles' Funeral Speech look like a Greek Version gone wrong, we kept our heads, for Ramsay had taught us how to handle a document.[1]

Another of Ramsay's pupils who has recently given some account of his performance as a teacher (the late Dr. Alexander Ross, until recently Associate Editor of *The Evangelical Quarterly*) describes the occasion when Ramsay's knighthood was announced.

---

1 W. M. Calder and J. Fraser, *Aberdeen University Review*, March 1934, pp. 104 f.

The news of the conferring of this honour reached us one morning in November 1906 and that morning the Latin classroom was crowded, all the available sitting and standing space being occupied, most of those present having forsaken their proper classes for the occasion. When the professor entered, there was a burst of vociferous cheering, handkerchiefs and note books being waved wildly in the air. When the deafening noise had at last been stilled, he was invited to make a speech. According to a newspaper report which I have before me, he said: "Ladies' and gentlemen (loud cheers), I am afraid I am detaining a large number of you from your classes (cries of 'No, no,' and 'not at all'). I am glad to see that for once you seem to enjoy the atmosphere of the Humanity classroom (cheers and cries of 'Oh, oh, Sir William') — as I am afraid that on many occasions it has been a place of terror (loud cries of 'No') — a vale of tears, through which you had to pass on your pilgrimage through this University." Later on, there was an allusion to the students who, by carving their names on the desks, planned to leave "a memorial of their former presence on these benches for future generations to discover." At this point a voice called out "excavations!" — a manifest reference to far more important excavations in Asia Minor.[2]

Mr. Gasque's study, however, is concerned with Ramsay's contributions to New Testament study. These were many-sided and valuable. He had received no biblical or theological training, but he acquired, by dint of his painstaking archaeological research coupled with his mastery of first-century literature, an unrivalled knowledge of the historical and geographical background of the apostolic age, especially where Asia Minor was concerned, and he used that knowledge effectively to illuminate the New Testament. The nineteenth-century Ramsay was a very great man; if even then he was inclined to overstate his case, at least he had a good case to overstate. The twentieth-century Ramsay suffered in his scholarly reputation because he allowed himself to be persuaded by Sir William Robertson Nicoll to don the mantle of a popular apologist. That Ramsay was no "fundamentalist" is evident to any careful reader of that section of *St. Paul the Traveller* which deals with the first five chapters of Acts, but this section comes near the end of the book, and probably a large proportion of his devout reading public never got so far. It is no disgrace for a scholar to obtain a reputation as a defender of the faith, but when this reputation is gained by covering reams of paper with apologetic material, spreading the factual content out as thin as possible to make it go farther, it is apt to be gained at the expense of his reputation for pure scholarship. The twentieth-century Ramsay tended to be dismissed as unworthy of serious attention by many *Neutestamentler* who never made themselves acquainted with the solid achievements of the nineteenth-century Ramsay, which underlay his

2 A. Ross, *Monthly Record of the Free Church of Scotland*, April 1962, p. 69.

more popular work of later years. Whatever may be thought of the superstructure, the foundation was always sound, and even in his most ill-considered work one constantly comes across flashes of insight and original contributions to knowledge which one would not willingly have missed. A quarter of a century after his death the time is opportune for a reassessment of his work, and I am glad to commend Mr. Gasque's reassessment to readers who have a concern for New Testament scholarship.

F. F. BRUCE

PREFACE

One of the surprising facts in the history of New Testament criticism is the small amount of attention that has been given to the work of Sir William Mitchell Ramsay (1851-1939). In the preface to the second edition of his commentary on the Greek text of Acts, Prof. F. F. Bruce remarked that he is "repeatedly amazed by modern writers who deal with areas of New Testament scholarship to which Ramsay made contributions of peculiar value, with hardly so much as a hint that such a person ever lived."[1] Writing twelve years later, Bishop Stephen Neill also observed this continued neglect.[2] As far as I have been able to determine, the only study hitherto which has been devoted to an account of his life and work is a brief essay by W. F. Howard, first published in the journal *Religion in Life* in 1939 and later reprinted as a chapter in his book *The Romance of New Testament Scholarship*.[3]

My introduction to Ramsay came in a college course in biblical archaeology. Since my first reading, I have become a devotee. My interest in his work was heightened by a brief visit to Asiatic Turkey and the cities of Paul in the summer of 1962.

In his above-mentioned essay Howard suggests that

> it would be a fine discipline for a young scholar, who wishes to specialize in New Testament studies, to go through Ramsay's published books and to compile a careful index of all Greek words dealt with, and another of all subject-matter that concerns the New Testament and early Christian history.[4]

I may be the first person to have taken up his challenge; at least, I am the first person to have done so and to publish the results. I have sought to make a careful study of all of Ramsay's books and most of his published articles that relate to the study of the New Testament, and I have included as appendices lists of the most important subjects, Scripture references, and Greek words and phrases which he has treated in his major works.[5] I have also appended an essay by Ramsay describing a typical summer's exploration in Asia Minor.[6]

---

1 *The Acts of the Apostles* (2nd ed.; London: Tyndale Press, 1952), p. viii.
2 *The Interpretation of the New Testament 1861-1961* (London: Oxford University Press, 1964), pp. 142-146.
3 (London: Epworth Press, 1949), pp. 138-155.
4 *Romance*, pp. 154-155.
5 See Appendices II-IV.
6 See Appendix V.

I wish to express my appreciation to those who have helped me in my work: Prof. Everett F. Harrison, of Fuller Theological Seminary, under whose supervision this study was written and presented as a thesis as a part of the requirements for the Master of Theology degree; Prof. F. F. Bruce, Rylands Professor of Biblical Criticism and Exegesis, University of Manchester, whose two commentaries on Acts have been helpful guides in my appreciation of Ramsay, who has read my manuscript and has graciously written the foreword; the librarian of Aberdeen University, Dr. W. D. Simpson, who has helped by supplying both bibliographical and biographical information; Dr. Wilbur M. Smith, who shared his enthusiasm for Ramsay, provided valuable biographical information, and gave me access to his latest book, in which he has included a little-known sermon by Ramsay; Prof. William Sanford LaSor, of Fuller Theological Seminary, and Prof. Bastiaan Van Elderen, of Calvin Theological Seminary, who read my manuscript and encouraged me to have it published; my friends and colleagues, Messrs. Donald Tinder, Clifford Christians, Donald Hagner, Murray Harris, Paul E. Leonard, and Colin Hemer, who have read the typescript and have given the author numerous helpful suggestions for its improvement; and my wife, Laurel, without whose patience and encouragement this study could never have been written.

W. W. G.

Manchester, England
November 1965

LIST OF ABBREVIATIONS[1]

1 Excepting HDB, all works are by Ramsay. Complete bibliographical data is given in the bibliography at the end the book.

BRD   *The Bearing of Recent Discovery on the Trustworthiness of the New Testament,* 1915.

CB   *The Cities and Bishoprics of Phrygia,* 1895 and 1897.

CRE   *The Church in the Roman Empire before A.D. 170,* 1893.

CSP   *The Cities of St. Paul: Their Influence on His Life and Thought,* 1907.

EC   *The Education of Christ: Hill-Side Reveries,* 1902.

FCC   *The First Christian Century: Notes on Dr. Moffatt's Introduction to the Literature of the New Testament,* 1911.

HCG   *A Historical Commentary on St. Paul's Epistle to the Galatians,* 1899.

HDB   James Hastings (ed.), *Dictionary of the Bible,* 1898-1904.

HG   *The Historical Geography of Asia Minor,* 1890.

LP   *Luke the Physician and Other Studies in the History of Religion,* 1908.

LSC   *The Letters to the Seven Churches of Asia,* 1904.

PAC   *Pictures of the Apostolic Church: Studies in the Book of Acts,* 1910.

POS   *Pauline and Other Studies in Early Christian History,* 1906.

SPT   *St. Paul the Traveller and the Roman Citizen,* 1895.

TP   *The Teachings of Paul in Terms of the Present Day,* 1913.

WCB   *Was Christ Born at Bethlehem?* 1898.

I

AN INTRODUCTION TO THE MAN
AND HIS WORK

In the person of Sir William Ramsay (1851-1939) one finds a rare combination. He was, on the one hand, a classical scholar and archaeologist, "the foremost authority of his day on the topography, antiquities, and history of Asia Minor in ancient times"[1]; at the same time he was one of the foremost authorities in the study of the New Testament, especially the Book of Acts and the letters of Paul. Few men are able to become masters in one field of study; Ramsay was master in two.

William Mitchell Ramsay was born the youngest son of a third-generation lawyer in Glasgow, Scotland, on March 15, 1851. His father passed away when he was six years old. Shortly thereafter the family moved from the city of Glasgow to the family home in the country district near Alloa.

His older brother and maternal uncle, Andrew Mitchell, made it possible for him to have the best education attainable. He received excellent preparation for university at the Aberdeen Gymnasium and from there went on to study at the University of Aberdeen, where he achieved high distinction.

In March, 1868, at the end of his second year at the university, he was enjoying his college work immensely and finding every moment spent in classwork or in preparation a delight. Of this time he later wrote, "The idea was simmering unconsciously in my mind that scholarship was the life for me: not the life of teaching, which was repellent, but the life of discovery."[2] When

---

1 J. G. C. Anderson, "Sir William Mitchell Ramsay," *Dictionary of National Biography 1931-1940*, p. 727.
2 BRD, p. 7.

the final day of the school term arrived, the members of the second-year class were all gathered in the Latin classroom. Ramsay later remarked that he had the feeling that something significant was going to happen that morning. Both the Professor of Greek and the Professor of Latin announced to the class that he was the number one student in each subject. Then and there his life was determined; he formed the resolve to be a scholar and to make everything else in his life subservient to that purpose and career.[3] Forty-five years later, he looked back on that day:

> In the class-room, also, one other matter settled itself. The border-land between Greece and the East, the relation of Greek literature to Asia, had already a vague fascination for me; and this was to be the direction of the life that I imagined in the future. As it turned out that thought of the relation between Greece and the East was an anticipation of my life; but the form developed in a way that I did not imagine until many years passed. I thought of work in a room or a library, but it has lain largely in the open air and on the geographical frontier where Greek-speaking people touched the East. I thought of Greek literature in its relation to Asia; but the subject widened into the relation between the spirit of Europe and of Asia through the centuries.[4]

How was he to achieve his goal to be a scholar? He knew the only path lay in an Oxford Fellowship, so before the meeting ended he had made his plans in that direction. However, he was careful to tell no one but his closest friends, for his family had intended that he compete for an appointment in the Indian Civil Service. When he finally did tell them three years after that memorable day in March, there was strong disapproval on the part of some; they thought it was foolish to turn to a life of scholarship with its vague uncertainties. But in 1872, the year following his graduation, he began what turned out to be five years of study at Oxford University with the aid of an Aberdeen graduate scholarship and another scholarship from St. John's College, Oxford. Here he received further academic honors.

During the course of his second year at Oxford, he was enabled by his uncle to spend a time studying Sanskrit at the University of Göttingen, Germany, under the great scholar, Theodor Benfey. This experience was, in his own words, a critical event in his life.

> Then for the first time, under the tuition of Professor Theodor Benfey, I came into close relations with a great scholar of the modern type, and gained some insights into modern methods of literary investigation; and my thoughts have ever since turned towards the border lands between European and Asiatic civilization.[5]

He later wrote of this experience:

---

3 BRD, pp. 9-10.
4 BRD, p. 10.
5 Letter of dedication to Andrew Mitchell, Esq., appended to first edition of SPT.

The way of scholarship had been hitherto arid in my education, the sense of discovery was never quickened, and the power of perceiving truth was becoming atrophied. Scholarship had been a learning of opinions, and not a process of gaining real knowledge. One learned what others had thought, but not what truth was. Benfey was a vivifying wind, to breathe life into dry bones, for he showed scholarship as discovery and not as a rehearsing of wise opinions.[6]

Further inspiration was received from Henry Jardine Bidder, of St. John's College, Oxford, "who first opened his eyes to the true spirit of Hellenism and so helped to fit him for the work which he had in view."[7]

In July, 1879, while vacationing in Scotland with his recently acquired wife, he received a letter from Mr. Stuart Poole, Keeper of the Coins in the British Museum, telling of a travelling studentship offered by Exeter College, Oxford, for three years' "travel and research in the Greek lands"; Mr. Poole advised Ramsay that he should come to the museum and study in preparation for it. The letter mentioned one other outstanding candidate for the award, a recent graduate of Trinity College, Dublin. That candidate turned out to be the later famous scholar, critic, dramatist, and poet, Oscar Wilde. Ramsay won the scholarship; and, being advised by Sir Charles Newton of the British Museum to go to the west coast of Asia Minor rather than to Athens, he and his yohng wife set off for Smyrna (now Izmir). There they landed early in May of 1880.

At Smyrna he met Sir Charles Wilson, who was then British consul-general in Anatolia and an experienced explorer. Wilson gave him helpful advice concerning the exploration of the unknown inland regions of the country, and he invited him to accompany him on two long journeys into the interior. This gave him his first opportunity to study the geography and archaeology of Roman proconsular Asia, Phrygia, Lycaonia, Cappadocia, and Galatia at firsthand and to begin an exploration that was continued, except for one break (1891-1899),[8] until 1914, and to embark on a long life of devotion to Anatolian studies.

We are given two interesting portraits of Ramsay the archaeologist at work by two of his fellow workers. The first is from *The Accidents of an Antiquary's Life*, the autobiography of D. G. Hogarth, another great archaeologist.

6 BRD, p. 13.
7 Anderson, *op. cit.*, p. 727.
8 An attack of cholera, contracted on a ship coming from Alexandretta, Turkey, incapacitated him for these years; during this time he aimed at finding and financing a successor rather than continuing his field work himself. He found a successor in a pupil of his earliest years at Aberdeen, J. G. C. Anderson, later Professor of Classical Art and Archaeology at Oxford. BRD, p. 29.

The apparatus of travel, which we gathered in Smyrna, was of the simplest — a single tent and a few pots and pans, but no canned stores; and two simple villagers were hired to serve us. The qualifications of the one chosen to cook became manifest on the second night in camp. We had left railhead at Seraikeuy, and ridden up the Lycus valley to the foot of the white cliffs of Hierapolis. Mehmet bought a turkey of the peasants of Pambuk Kalessi, and was bidden to have it ready for the next night's supper. Early on the morrow we went up to the site, and all that day, under a broiling sun and among some of the best-preserved Roman tombs in Asia Minor, I entered on an arduous apprenticeship to the best epigraphist in Europe. Sharpset at nightfall we hurried down, expectant of our turkey. Mehmet sat placid, the bird at his feet. It was a corpse, indeed, but no more, not even a plucked one. "What am I to do with this?" said Mehmet. He learned better as time went on; but throughout that journey we had little except sodden messes to eat, faring worse than any traveller need fare. It was partly because our leader cared little for what he ate, but more because, like his followers, he journeyed on a slender purse. Ramsay had made to himself a European reputation as an explorer of Asia Minor at a cost which another man would think scarcely sufficient for the tour of Germany; and it had become his principle, as, for similar reasons, it has become Petrie's, to suffer none but the barest means to his end. If both have pushed their practice to exceeding discomfort, both have taught several young Britons how little is necessity and how much superfluity; and it is not the least of my many debts to Ramsay that I gained in my first tour of exploration the will and the capacity to go farther at less cost than perhaps anyone but my master.[9]

The second picture is a description of Ramsay at work from two letters of Miss Gertrude Bell, who shared some of his travels and researches.

Madan Shehar
May 25, 1907

The Ramsays arrived yesterday. I was in the middle of digging up a Church, when suddenly two carts hove into sight and there they were. It was about three in the afternoon. They instantly got out, refused to think of going to the tents, Lady R. made tea (for they were starving) in the open, and R. oblivious of all other considerations was at once lost in the problems the Church presented. It was too delightful to have someone as much excited about it as I was. . . .

Daile
June 8, 1907

We are getting so much material that it will certainly make a book. Our plan is that Sir W. shall write the historic and epigraphic part and I the architectural. It will be worth doing, for this is the first time that an accurate study has been made of any one district in these parts; hitherto people have only travelled through and seen what they could see and gone on. . . . I should have been helpless without Sir W., and the more I work with him the more I like him and respect his knowledge. In fact, it is being a magnificent success, quite everything I hoped it would be.[10]

9 Quoted in W. F. Howard, *The Romance of New Testament Scholarship* (London: Epworth Press, 1949), pp. 143-144.
10 Quoted in Stephen Neill, *The Interpretation of the New Testament 1861-1961* (London: Oxford University Press, 1964), p. 141.

In 1885 Ramsay became the first Professor of Classical Art and Archaeology at Oxford. The following year he was appointed Regius Professor of Humanity, as the Latin professorship is called, at his alma mater, the University of Aberdeen. There he remained until his retirement in 1911.[11]

Ramsay was knighted in 1906 on the occasion of the four hundredth anniversary of the founding of the University of Aberdeen for his distinguished service to the scholarly world. In addition to this honor he received many other academic distinctions in his lifetime. He was recipient of three honorary fellowships from Oxford colleges (Exeter in 1898, Lincoln in 1899, and St. John's in 1912), and he was honored by doctorates from nine universities: Oxford, St. Andrews, Glasgow, Aberdeen, Cambridge, Edinburgh, New York, Bordeaux, and Marburg. He was one of the original members of the British Academy and an honorary member of just about every scholarly association devoted to archaeological and historical research. In 1893 he was awarded the Gold Medal of Pope Leo XIII and in 1906 the Victoria Medal of the Royal Geographical Society. His travels took him not only to Turkey, but also to the great universities of the world for lectures; he visited America on three occasions (1894, 1910, and 1913) for special lectures at leading universities and seminaries.[12]

According to his obituary notice in *The Times* (London),

> Ramsay's abiding fame will rest first on his comprehensive exploration of Asia Minor; ... and secondly, on the new method which he developed and taught to students of ancient geography. On account of both he received worldwide recognition.[13]

In his work in Asia Minor he was concerned primarily with the problem of geographical identification. When he first began, very few historical places could be identified with any certainty, especially in the interior.

> Taking into his purview sites of all periods down to the Byzantine, he sought the help of evidence neglected or little used before, notably that of local coin types, and that of Christian authors and legends, and set out to interpret the ancient geography of Asia Minor by noting the relative positions of points on roads and by applying the method of exclusion to administrative groups of towns, of which some members were already fixed with fair certainty in the map.[14]

---

11 Howard, *Romance*, p. 139, suggests that Ramsay retired due to ill health. If this is correct, he certainly recovered quickly, for he was active as a writer and lecturer until the end of his life. In a personal letter to the author, Professor F. F. Bruce suggests that he was able to retire at the rather early age of sixty due to the steady income derived from the publication of his books — which went through many editions — by Hodder and Stoughton. "In those days there was no fixed retirement age for Scottish professors, who were appointed *ad vitam aut culpam*, and some went on into their eighties!"
12 Anderson, *op. cit.*, pp. 727-728.
13 April 22, 1939, p. 14.
14 *Ibid.*

This was combined with extensive exploration and excavation throughout the south-central part of the sub-continent.

In the year of his first visit to Asia Minor (1879), Ramsay contributed about one hundred articles on classical subjects to the ninth edition of the *Encyclopaedia Britannica;* most of these were too short to have a signature. At the very beginning of his exploration Ramsay made a name for himself by publishing the results of his discoveries in various European scholarly journals, most notably the *Journal of Hellenic Studies.* Because his articles were scattered throughout so many different periodicals, the French archaeologist Perrot was moved to sigh, "What trouble Ramsay would have spared us all by writing one book!"[15] That book came at last when his monumental work on *The Historical Geography of Asia Minor*[16] was published by the Royal Geographical Society in 1890.

This work did not appear, however, without a great deal of labor and discouragement. Ramsay explains in his preface:

> In May, 1886, the first sketch of it was read before the Society. The difficulty of the subject, and the distraction caused by other work both as a Professor (first in Oxford and afterwards in Aberdeen), and as a traveller (I left London for Smyrna the day after reading the paper, and spent considerable part of the summer of 1886, 1887, and 1888 in Asia Minor), delayed the completion and publication of the sketch. In the beginning of April, 1888, I brought the complete MS. with me to London to hand over to the printer. I discovered, thirty-six hours after starting from Aberdeen, that the manscript was no longer in the bag where I had placed it, and which had been for the most of the time close to my hand, and I have never found the slightest clue to the time or manner of its loss.... All notes for it had been destroyed....[17]

This would have crushed a lesser man. Ten years of research gone! Yet Ramsay did his best to rewrite the book and even added a second part, which included a collection of new material for the history and antiquities of the area. Even though the rewritten book — on the author's confession — was a less finished work than the original had been, it marked an epoch in the study of ancient geography and established Ramsay's prominence in the field. *The Historical Geography* is foundational for all later study in the history and geography of Asia Minor.

The presupposition of all Ramsay's work is this:

> Topography is the foundation of history. No one who has familiarized himself with Attic history in books and has afterwards ascended Pentelicus and seen that history spread forth before him in the valleys and mountains and sea that have moulded it will ever disbelieve in the value

---

15 *The Times* (London), April 22, 1939, p. 14.
16 Royal Geographical Society, Supplementary Papers, Vol. 4 (London: John Murray, 1890; repr. Amsterdam: Adolph M. Hakkert, 1962).
17 HG, p 3.

of topography as an aid to history. . . . If we want to understand the Ancients, especially the Greeks, we must breathe the same air as they did and saturate ourselves with the same scenery and the same nature that wrought upon them. For this end correct topography is a necessary though humble servant.[18]

And this is exactly what Sir William Ramsay did: he saturated himself with the geography and history of the Graeco-Roman world. He always insisted upon originality in research and first-hand acquaintance with the facts. Throughout his life he had little time for those who would assume the position of authorities on the history and geography of Asia Minor or the missionary travels of the Apostle Paul without having a firsthand acquaintance with the facts of the matter.

Two things characterize Ramsay above all else. He was original and he was thorough. He writes this in the introduction to his *Historical Geography:*

My scheme has been (after several experiences of the difficulties caused by accepting wrong conjectures of modern writers) to make an absolutely fresh work founded on the ancient authorities alone, in which the geographical situation, the natural surroundings and the commercial advantages of each city should be set forth in an account of its history.[19]

Ninety-five per cent of the references made to ancient writers in his work, the reader is assured, were found by the author in his own perusal of the original authorities, most of whom were read several times in the original.[20] This is quite a feat, for he quotes from ninety different ancient writers, from classical historians to early church fathers, in both Greek and Latin.

Ramsay's *Historical Geography* is divided into two parts. The first is entitled, "General Principles," and the second, "A Sketch of the Historical Geography of the Various Provinces." Part one begins with a discussion of the conflict between Orientalism and Hellenism in Asia Minor. His observations here laid the foundation for much further thought on the matter culminating in his Gifford Lectures in the University of Edinburgh for 1915-1916.[21] The very character of the plateau as a borderland between the East and the West has, according to Ramsay, marked it out as a battleground between the Oriental and European spirit.

The idea of this great struggle was a formative principle which moulded the gradual development of the Iliad, and gave the tone to Herodotus's epic history. We can trace its main features from that time onwards. Greece and Persia were the representative antagonists for two centuries. Then the conquests of Alexander, organized and consolidated later by the genius of Rome, made the European spirit apparently victorious for many centuries.

---

18 *HG.* pp. 51-52.
19 *HG*, p. 6.
20 *HG*, pp. 6-7.
21 *Asianic Elements in Greek Civilization* (London: John Murray, 1927).

But the conquest was not real. Romans governed Asia Minor because, with their marvellous governing talent, they knew how to adapt their administration to the people of the plateau. It is true that the great cities put on a western appearance, and took Latin or Greek names; Latin and Greek were the languages of government, of the educated classes, and of polite society. Only this superficial aspect is attested in literature and in ordinary history, and when I began to travel the thought never occurred to me that there was any other. The conviction has gradually forced itself on me that the real state of the country was very different. Greek was not the popular language of the plateau even in the third century after Christ: the mass of people spoke Lycaonian, and Galatian, and Phrygian, although those who wrote books wrote Greek, and those who governed spoke Latin. The people continued to believe in their own religion, their gods were identified by educated persons with the gods of Greece and Rome, and called by Greek names; but they had none of the Greek or Roman character, they were Asiatic deities. Christianity conquered the land, and succeeded in doing what Greece and Rome had never done: it imposed its language on the people. But the Christianity of Phrygia was never like the Christianity of Europe. . . .
The foundation of Constantinople was a sign that the West had not really conquered Asia Minor.[22]

He carries on with an important discussion of the great roads and trade routes of ancient Anatolia, from the so-called "Royal Road" of the Persian period to the Byzantine roads, which were the basis of the modern Turkish road system. He discusses the value of the various ancient geographical authorities for Asia Minor and concludes with an important note on the change of site of ancient cities. In part two, after a brief general introduction to the area as a whole, he goes through the various provinces, city by city, listing all of the available geographical and historical information that he has been able to uncover in the study of historical sources and in his extensive explorations. The order is to a great extent the order of discovery. This, together with the limits of Professor Ramsay's travels (principally in Asia, Phrygia, Galatia, Lycaonia, and Cappadocia), prevents the book from being a full-fledged and systematic discussion of the historical geography of Asia Minor as a whole — as the title might indicate.

The second great work Ramsay produced in the area of archaeology was the monumental volume, *The Cities and Bishoprics of Phrygia*.[23] This is described in the sub-title as "an essay of the local history of Phrygia from the earliest times to the Turkish conquest." The work was intended to be a multi-volumed work, but only one volume (in two parts) was completed due to lack of evidence. The first part, published in 1895, surveys those

22 HG, pp. 24-25.
23 (Oxford: Clarendon Press, 1895, Vol. 1, pt. 1; 1897, Vol. 1, pt. 2).

cities in the area of the Lycus (Lycos) River valley; Laodicea, Hierapolis, Colossae, and other less important cities. The second part, published in 1897, covers the cities of west and west-central Phrygia, the most important of which are Eumereia and Apameia. This latter section includes two important chapters on early Christian inscriptions and one on the Jews in Phrygia. Basing his argument on a tradition of the Talmud, he argues that the Jews of this region were generally absorbed into the Christian church at an early date.[24]

Perhaps the least known of Sir William Ramsay's contributions to the study of ancient history and geography are the articles he wrote for the five volumes of Hastings' *Dictionary of the Bible* between 1898 and 1904. These are sixty-three in number and deal primarily with cities and geographical terms of Greece and Asia Minor.[25] The two most important in this series are the extensive essays in the extra volume on the "Religion of Greece and Asia Minor."[26] and "Roads and Travel in the New Testament."[27] The first of these begins with the primitive Anatolian and pre-Hellenic religion and carries the story down to the Christian era; it includes valuable sections on the cult of the Great Mother, the mysteries, and the attitude of St. Paul to Greek philosophy. The second answers just about any questions one would have about travel in the time of the New Testament and includes two excellent maps, the first tracing the most important routes by land and sea in the Roman Empire and the second covering Asia Minor in detail.

Under the general category of archaeology one should mention the three articles contributed to the volume written by Ramsay and six of his early students for the quatercentenary of the University of Aberdeen,[28] the publication of the results of

---

24 *CB, part* 1, pp. 674-676. However, according to Jastrow's *Dictionary of the Talmud,* the reference is not to Phrygia, but to Prugitha, a district in Northern Palestine known for its wine.
25 Cf. Appendix I.
26 *HDB,* extra vol., pp. 109-156.
27 *HDB,* extra vol., pp. 375-402.
28 "Preliminary Report to the Wilson Trustees on Exploration in Phrygia and Lycaonia," "The War of Moslem and Christian for the Possession of Asia Minor," "The Tekmoreian Guest-Friend: An Anti-Christian Society on the Imperial Estates at Pisidian Antioch," in William M. Ramsay (ed.), *Studies in the History and Art of the Eastern Provinces of the Roman Empire* (Aberdeen: Aberdeen University Press, 1906), pp. 231-377. The influence of Ramsay in inspiring research in Asia Minor can be seen from this quotation from the preface: "We venture to lay before the University and the distinguished guests, both strangers and graduates, who come to greet its entrance on the fifth century of work, a sample of the research that has been performed in one line alone of classical study by its students. It was the writer's wish to compile a bibliography of Asia Minor exploration during the last twenty-seven years . . . but this volume could not have appeared in time if the compilation had been included. The bibliography would show in statistics that, notable as have been the writings in that department of a series of excellent scholars, many of whose names are now household words in the world of learning, *the bulk at any rate of the work of Aberdeen graduates in the department equals the bulk of all the rest,* even taking into account the stately German folios on Pergamon, Lycia, etc., and the beautiful French volumes on Myrina" (pp. ix-x, italics mine).

his and Miss Gertrude Bell's excavation of the "Thousand and One Churches" (actually only about 28 — a typical example of Oriental exaggeration!) in the region of Kara Dagh (Black Mountain),[29] and his Gifford Lectures on the *Asianic Elements in Greek Civilization*. The end of his life found him laboring on an extensive work on *The Social Basis of Roman Power in Asia Minor,* edited and published posthumously by his former student, Professor J. G. C. Anderson of Oxford.[30]

This survey of the work of Sir William Ramsay, the historian and archaeologist, could not be concluded without focusing attention upon what is probably the best popular essay on the historical geography of Asia Minor ever written. This appeared in *The National Geographic Magazine* in 1922 under the title, "A Sketch of the Geographical History of Asia Minor."[31] It began with this excellent description of Asia Minor:

> In shape the peninsula of Asia Minor may be compared by a rough analogy to the right hand laid palm upward, with the fingers pointing to the west. The palm is the central plateau, which is surrounded with a rim of mountains. Like fingers, five chains of mountains extend from the plateau, most of them stretching far out into the Aegean Sea, as if they were trying to force their way to Europe.
>
> These mountain chains are continued by chains of islands, which form, as it were, stepping-stones for the march of a giant from Asia to Europe.[32]

29 Sir William M. Ramsay and Miss Gertrude L. Bell, *The Thousand and One Churches* (London: Hodder and Stoughton, 1909).
30 (Aberdeen: Aberdeen University Press, 1941). Ramsay had evidently made an agreement with Professor J. R. S. Sterrett (d. 1914), of Cornell University, to make use of some of his discoveries and to publish the results in this work.
31 42 (Nov. 1922): 553-570.
32 *Ibid.*, p. 553.

II

LUKE THE HISTORIAN

Although it was as an archaeologist and a geographer that Ramsay did his most substantial work, this is regarded merely as foundational for the purpose of this book. His firsthand investigation into the antiquities of Asia Minor provides the background for his study of the New Testament. The immense amount of knowledge that he had accumulated in the study of the historical and geographical condition of the Roman provinces in Asia Minor was later brought to bear on the interpretation of the New Testament. And it is as a New Testament scholar that we now want to look at him.

Any discussion of Sir William Ramsay and the New Testament must begin with the Book of Acts, because it is here that he first became interested in the study of the New Testament, and it is here that he made his most significant contribution.

During Ramsay's days as a university student, the study of apostolic history was dominated by Ferdinand Christian Baur (1792-1860) and his so-called Tübingen School. Reading Acts and the letters of Paul in the light of the Hegelian dialectic interpretation of history and the assumption that only four Pauline epistles were undoubtedly genuine (Galatians, Romans, 1 and 2 Corinthians), they radically altered the traditional understanding of New Testament history. They saw in the early church two opposing elements (thesis and antithesis) represented by Peter and Paul; in Acts they found the reconciliation (synthesis) of these two parties in the Catholic Church of the second century. Their conclusions demanded a very late date for most of the New Testament writings, especially Acts.[1]

When he first began his work in Asia Minor, Ramsay's views concerning the Book of Acts were under the influence of this school of thought. "I had read a good deal of modern criticism about the book," he wrote,

> and dutifully accepted the current opinion that it was written during the second half of the second century by an author who wished to influence the minds of people in his own time by a highly wrought and imaginative description of the early Church. His object was not to present a trustworthy picture of facts in the period of about A.D. 50, but to produce a certain effect on his own time by setting forth a carefully coloured account of events and persons of that older period. He wrote for his contemporaries, not for truth. He cared nought for geographical or historical surroundings of the period A.D. 30 to 60. He thought only of the period A.D. 160-180, and how he might paint the heroes of old times in situations that should touch the conscience of his contemporaries. Antiquarian or geographical truth was less than valueless in a design like this: one who thought of such things was distracting his attention from the things that really mattered, the things that would move the minds of men in the second century.[2]

In his search for information bearing on the geography and history of Asia Minor he at first paid slight attention to the early Christian authorities. He had gained the impression in his studies that these were quite unworthy of consideration for a historian; anything having to do with religion belonged to the realm of the theologians, not that of the historians. When he spent time copying Christian inscriptions in his earliest years of travel, he felt the time to be wasted — even though a sense of duty compelled him to make copies of them. Finally, in a desperate search for any information of a geographical and antiquarian nature, he began to study the journeys of Paul in this region of the world as described in the Book of Acts. He hardly expected to find any information of value regarding the condition of Asia Minor in the time of Paul; rather, he thought he would find material bearing upon the second half of the second century of the Christian era, i.e. the age (he thought) in which the author of Acts lived.

In his book, *The Bearing of Recent Discovery on the Trustworthiness of the New Testament,* Ramsay tells how he came to

---

1 In the Tübingen School, cf. J. Haussleiter, "Ferdinand Christian Baur and the Later Tübingen School," *The New Schaff-Herzog Encyclopaedia of Religious Knowledge,* edited by S. M. Jackson et al. (New York: Funk and Wagnals, 1908), 2:7-11; A. C. McGiffert, "The Historical Criticism of Acts in Germany," *The Beginnings of Christianity,* edited by S. M. Jackson et al. (New York: Funk and Wagnalls, 1908), 2:7-11; A. C. McGiffert, 2:367-395; Neill, *Interpretation,* pp. 19-28.

2 BRD, pp. 37-38.

change his mind on the subject.[3] The first thing that caused him to begin to doubt the conclusion which he had assumed was a careful study of Acts 14:5-12. Here it is said that Paul and Barnabas, on account of an angry mob, fled from Iconium "to Lystra and Derbe, cities of Lycaonia, and the surrounding region" (v. 6). In these words it is implied that the apostles crossed over a frontier into Lycaonia; that is, that the border of Lycaonia lay between the cities of Iconium and Lystra, and that Iconium did not belong to the country called Lycaonia.

Now, it was formerly assumed in modern treatises on ancient geography that Iconium was a city of Lycaonia. This passage in the fourteenth chapter of Acts was thought of as a typical example of the lack of local exactitude by the author of Acts, who was writing at a much later date than the events he was narrating. Assuming that Iconium was a city of Lycaonia, then to speak of going from Iconium into Lycaonia would be the same as if someone today were to speak of going from Chicago into Illinois, or from London to England. The impression left upon the mind is that "this detail of the journey of Paul and Barnabas was deliberately invented by the writer (who was under the false impression about the situation of Iconium and the frontier)...."[4]

However, as Ramsay went on to demonstrate conclusively,[5] this is not, in point of fact, the case. Iconium was not a part of Lycaonia; rather, it belonged to Phrygia, an entirely different district of Asia Minor. The people were of a different stock, and they spoke a different language from that of the Lycaonians. Once this fact is realized, the narrative of Acts 14 comes to life with local color and detailed accuracy as to the actual situation. Rather than the narrative bearing the stamp of a historical fiction, it becomes plausible that the account is based upon personal experience and that Paul himself could be the source behind the account. Facts incidental to the story, such as crossing the border between Phrygia and Lycaonia (v. 6) and the speech of the people of Lystra being in the Lycaonian tongue (v. 11), point in this direction. The fact that, once inside the border of Lycaonia, Paul and Barnabas were safe from the Iconium mob and the contrast between the Phrygian language and that which they heard upon their arrival at Lystra would have impressed these incidents upon their minds. Futhermore, Ramsay goes on to note the connection between Zeus and Hermes as associated gods

3 pp. 39-52. Full bibliographical data for Ramsay's books of a biblical nature will be found in the bibliography at the end of the book.
4 BRD, p. 41.
5 Cf. BRD, pp. 53-78.

in this region as a further demonstration of the authenticity of the narrative.

This may sound like a small point to the uninitiated, but it is a very important one in the thought of Ramsay. The inference of these facts led him to conclude that this passage in Acts is meticulously accurate in regard to its professed historical setting.

> The boundaries mentioned are true to the period in which the action lies: they are not placed through the mistaken application by a later author of ancient statements to a time when they ceased to be pertinent: they are based on information given by an eye-witness, a person who had been engaged in the action described. The reader, if he reads the narrative rightly, can see with the eyes and hear with the ears of a man who was there and witnessed all that happened.[6]

The conclusion that slowly forced itself upon Ramsay was the exact opposite of the one he had hitherto assumed in regard to Acts. And if the theory to which he had committed himself could not be relied upon in respect to this one detail, he surmised that it evidently could not be relied upon in other details without being thoroughly tested. To state it more positively, if the author proves to be carefully accurate in a matter of one detail, would it not be likely that he would prove to be the same in regard to others?

> There is a certain presumption that a writer who proves to be exact and correct in one point will show the same qualities in other matters. No writer is correct by mere chance, or accurate sporadically. He is accurate by virtue of a certain habit of mind. Some men are accurate by nature; some are by nature loose and inaccurate.[7]

His attitude towards the Book of Acts was now radically changed. Instead of assuming the book to be untrustworthy in regard to its avowed historical situation, he now began to approach Acts with an open mind that it might after all prove to be accurate in any given detail. He now realized, as F. F. Bruce has stated, that if an author's trustworthiness "is vindicated in points where he can be checked, we should not assume that he is less trustworthy where we cannot test his accuracy."[8] Ramsay would at least give the writer of Acts the benefit of the doubt.

He writes of his new outlook in *The Bearing of Recent Discovery*:

> In the special work on which I was engaged at the time, some fresh investigation of the case was indispensable. Good and safe evidence about Asia Minor in the Imperial time or earlier was urgently required by an explorer and discoverer. If I could find such evidence, and test it in the country, a long vista of profitable work opened itself before me.... If

---

6 *BRD*, p. 79.
7 *BRD*, p. 80.
8 *Acts*, p. 17.

Luke's narrative was trustworthy, it was for me exceptionally valuable, as giving evidence on a larger scale. There was nothing else like it. No other ancient traveller has left an account of the journeys which he made across Asia Minor [Xenophon gives little more than names and distances]; and if the narrative of Paul's travels rests on first-class authority, it placed in my hands a document of unique and exceptional value to guide my investigations. To determine the value of this narrative was a fundamental condition for my future work.[9]

Over the years the opinion gradually forced itself upon him that Luke's history of early Christian origins was unsurpassed for its accuracy.

Further study of Acts XIII.-XXI. showed that the book could bear the most minute scrutiny of an authority for the facts of the Aegean world, and that it was written with such judgement, skill, art, and perception of the truth as to be a model of historical statement.[10]

After more than thirty years of close study of the milieu of first-century Christianity, he penned these words:

The more I have studied the narrative of the Acts, and the more I have learned year after year about Graeco-Roman society and thoughts and fashions, and organization in those provinces, the more I admire and the better I understand. I set out to look for truth on the borderland where Greece and Asia meet, and found it here. You may press the words of Luke in a degree beyond any other historian's, and they stand the keenest scrutiny and the hardest treatment, provided always that the critic knows the subject and does not go beyond the limits of science and of justice.[11]

In the spring of 1892, Ramsay was invited to give six lectures at Mansfield College, Oxford. This gave him his first opportunity to set forth some of the views he had been developing concerning early Christian history. In the course of these lectures he dealt with the history of the church from A.D. 64 to 170, especially as regards the problem of persecution. When he published these lectures as *The Church in the Roman Empire before A.D. 170.* he added an introductory part covering the earliest stage of development. Here he first sought to articulate the development in his thoughts regarding the account of Paul's missionary journeys in Acts. From a comparison with his later works, one can observe that he was only beginning at this time to appreciate the great historical value of Acts. All he ventured to argue for was "that the narrative in Acts of Paul's journeys is founded on, actually incorporates, an account written under the immediate influence of Paul himself."[12]

The ideas found in seminal form in *The Church in the Roman Empire* are found fully developed in his *magnum opus, St. Paul*

---

9 *BRD*, pp. 81-82.
10 *BRD*, p. 85.
11 *BRD*, p. 89.
12 *CRE*, pp. 6-7.

the Traveller and the Roman Citizen, published first in 1895. This work established Ramsay's reputation as a Biblical scholar, as *The Historical Geography of Asia Minor* established him in the field of archaeology. It is in this work that Ramsay has undoubtedly made his greatest contribution to New Testament scholarship.

When he wrote the introductory chapters to *The Church in the Roman Empire,* he had no theory as to the date and composition of the Book of Acts. He was only concerned with one small part of the book — the travel narratives relating to Paul's missionary journeys. However, when he was invited to visit the United States two years later for lectures at Auburn Seminary (and incidentally at Harvard, Johns Hopkins, and Union Seminary, New York) , he had thoroughly worked through the whole of Acts and had come to a definite conclusion. He stated the view at which he had arrived in *St. Paul the Traveller* (the publication of his American lectures) :

> Our hypothesis is that *Acts* was written by a great historian, a writer who set himself to record the facts as they occurred, a strong partisan indeed, but raised above partiality by his perfect confidence that he had only to describe the facts as they occurred, in order to make the truth of Christianity and the honour of Paul apparent. . . . I shall argue that the book was composed by a personal friend and disciple of Paul, and if this be once established there will be no hesitation in accepting the primitive tradition that Luke was the author.[13]

The author of Acts is not to be regarded as the author of historical romance, legend, or third- or second-rate history. Rather he is the writer of an historical work of the highest order, a work to be compared with that of Thucydides, the greatest of the Greek historians.[14]

It is of greatest significance that Ramsay came to the study of Acts — and the rest of the New Testament — as a Roman historian rather than as a theologian. This is one factor that makes his books so fresh and so noteworthy. He did not come to prove a certain point of view; he simply aimed at an examination of the facts. Throughout the whole of his life he never held any theory as to the inerrancy of the Bible as a result of its special inspiration. His position in this regard is expressed in the following statement:

> In maintaining our hypothesis it is not necessary either to show that the author made no mistake, or to solve every difficulty. . . . We are making a historical and literary investigation. The greatest historians of

---

13 P. 14.
14 SPT, pp. 2-3.

other periods are not above error; and we may admit the possibility
that a first-century historian has made errors.[15]

He notes, further, that there remain many unsolved problems in
every ancient writer of value and that this is no less true of the
author of Acts. However, these problems do not detract from his
ability as a historian. One reason for our difficulty with Luke is
that his

> style is compressed to the highest degree; and he expects a great deal
> from the reader. He does not attempt to sketch the surroundings and
> set the whole scene like a picture before the reader; he states the bare
> facts that seem to him important, and leaves the reader to imagine the
> situation.[16]

A second problem was closely related in the thought of Ramsay to the problem of the reliability of Acts. Who are the
churches of Galatia to whom Paul writes and whom he addresses
as Galatians (Gal. 1:2; 3:1)? Is the reference to ethnic or political
Galatia? That is, does it signify the central mountainous region
of Asia Minor occupied by the descendants of the Gauls who
emigrated from Europe in the third century B.C.? Or does it refer to the Roman province of this name, which was a much
larger district (including "South Galatia")?

The question is involved with many problems and is still
vigorously debated today. The classic defender of the North
Galatian theory in Ramsay's day was J. B. Lightfoot (1828-1888),
the dean of Pauline scholars.[17] He argued that the natural meaning of the term would refer to the district which the Gauls inhabited. Furthermore, the main characteristics of the Gauls as a
people stand out in Paul's letter — especially their fickleness and
instability of character (Gal. 1:6, 3:1), and their concern for a
more external and ritualistic religion (Gal. 3:3).[18]

But the question may be asked, how does this fit in with Acts?
Acts speaks of Paul's extensive missionary activity in the South
Galatian region, i.e. in the cities of Pisidian Antioch, Iconium,
Lystra, and Derbe (Acts 13:14-14:23; 16:1-5), but we do not read
of any missionary work in North Galatia. Those who hold the
North Galatian theory point to two verses which refer (accord-
ing to this view) to Paul's evangelistic work in this region: Acts
16:6 and 18:23. The first of these reads:

15 *SPT*, p. 16.
16 *SPT*, p. 17.
17 *The Epistle of St. Paul to the Galatians* (Repr. Grand Rapids, Michigan: Zondervan
Publishing House, 1962), pp. 1-35.
18 *Ibid.*, pp. 13-17.

And they went through the region of Phrygia and Galatia, having been forbidden by the Holy Spirit to speak the word in Asia (RSV).

Διῆλθον δὲ τὴν Φρυγίαν καὶ Γαλατικὴν χώραν, κωλυθέντες ὑπὸ τοῦ Ἁγίου Πνεύματος λαλῆσαι τὸν λόγον ἐν τῇ Ἀσίᾳ.

And the second:

After spending some time there [in Syrian Antioch] he departed and went from place to place through the region of Galatia and Phrygia, strengthening all the disciples (RSV).

Καὶ ποιήσας χρόνον τινὰ ἐξῆλθεν, διερχόμενος καθεξῆς τὴν Γαλατικὴν χώραν καὶ Φρυγίαν, στηρίζων πάντας τοὺς μαθητάς.

The first of these references is taken by the exponents of the North Galatian hypothesis to refer to evangelistic activity conducted by Paul in the regions of (ethnic) Galatia and Phrygia. Great stress is laid upon the fact that τὴν Φρυγίαν καὶ Γαλατικὴν χώραν must refer to two distinct regions. Further, it is characteristic of Luke to use regional rather than political terms.

> Mysia, Phrygia, Pisidia, are all "geographical expressions" destitute of any political significance; and as they occur in the same parts of the narrative with Galatia, it seems fair to infer that the latter is similarly used.[19]

Moreover, Luke distinctly calls Lystra and Derbe cities of Lycaonia (13:6) and designates Antioch by the words "of Pisidia" (13:14) — all by geographical terms rather than by the provincial title of Galatia. James Moffatt argued that the word, διῆλθον, ("went through") meant not merely "transit across" but "transit with preaching activity"[20]; hence there is evidence that Paul may have established churches in this region.

Ramsay, however, was not satisfied with the traditional view. When he first began his study of the New Testament, he was guided by Lightfoot;[21] but the more he studied the facts as a Roman historian the more he became convinced that this theory just did not fit the facts. He confesses,

> To maintain this idea I had to reject the plain and natural interpretation of some passages; but when at last I found myself compelled to abandon it, and to understand Galatians as inhabitants of Roman Galatia, much that had been dark became clear, and some things that had seemed loose and vague became precise and definite.[22]

---

19 Lightfoot, Galatians, p. 19.
20 Introduction to the Literature of the New Testament (3rd ed. rev.; New York; Charles Scribner's Sons, 1922), p. 95.
21 CRE, pp. 8-9.
22 CRE, p. 9.

His views on the matter were first stated in *The Church in the
Roman Empire*[23] and further developed in *St. Paul the Traveller.*[24] In 1899 he published his *Historical Commentary on St.
Paul's Epistle to the Galatians;* here he gave this view its most
cogent expression.[25] The result has been that most British scholars (with the notable exception of Ramsay's faithful antagonist,
James Moffatt) have been impressed with the force of Ramsay's
arguments and have tended to accept the South Galatian theory.
German scholarship, with a few exceptions,[26] has maintained the
defense of the older view.

Several factors worked together to compel Ramsay to abandon
the North Galatian view. First, there was the marked difference
between the rustic Gaulish population of North Galatia, who
were probably little affected by Greek manners and language, and
the population of the cities, who were for the most part not
Gauls.[27] If Paul followed his custom and worked in the cities
(rather than the country district) of this area (assuming, for the
sake of argument, that he did do missionary work in North
Galatia), then his converts would have not for the most part been
Galatians in the ethnic sense; and to refer to them as Galatians
would be no more appropriate than in reference to the people
of the South Galatian area. Again, it was Paul's general practice
to work in cities that were generally Hellenized and where there
was a Jewish population; this would not have been the case, according to Ramsay's researches, in North Galatia in the first
century. Furthermore, there is little evidence for the existence of
Christianity in North Galatia until a quite late date. On the
other hand, a close study of the antiquities of the South Galatian
region convinced him that the simple name of Galatians would
be the ideal name to use in referring to the people of the cities of
Pisidian Antioch, Iconium, Lystra, and Derbe. In fact, it is the
only name that would be apropos to the situation.[28] They could
not be addressed as "the churches of Lycaonia" or "Lycaonians,"
because Antioch and Iconium were in the region of Phrygia.
Again, many of the inhabitants of these cities were not natives
to the region; therefore, the description of them as Lycaonian or
Phrygian would be quite inappropriate — especially since some of
the people would be Roman citizens (Antioch and Lystra were

---

23 Pp. 8-11, 16-111.
24 Pp. 89-151, 178-193.
25 Pp. 1-234.
26 For example, Theodore Zahn, *Introduction to the New Testament*, trans. from the
third German edition by J. M. Trout *et al.* (Repr. Grand Rapids, Mich.: Kregel Publica-
tions, 1953), 1:164-202.
27 Ramsay, "Galatia," *HDB*, 2:84.
28 Ramsay, "Galations," *HDB*, 2:91-92.

Roman colonies). Besides, the term Phrygian was a term with a very bad connotation and would not in good taste be used in referring to the people of that region. The only all-inclusive term available to use in speaking of the members of the churches that Paul founded in the region of South Galatia would be "Galatians," and he would naturally, as Romans, follow the Roman provincial divisions and ignore those national distinctions which were opposed to the organized Roman unity.[29] It was Paul's practice to use the titles of the Roman provinces in his letters, e.g., Achaia, Asia, and Macedonia. And it is significant that Paul refers to both Thessalonians and Philippians as "Macedonian" (2 Cor. 11:2, 4), when they actually belong to a geographical district whose indigenous people were called "Thracian."

One of the important factors leading Ramsay to the acceptance of the South Galatian Theory was a growing conviction concerning the nature of Luke as a historian. Now, one of the determining factors in the character of a historian is his selection of topics. "Does he show the true historian's power of seizing the great facts, and marking clearly the development of his subject?"[30] Ramsay was impressed more and more that one finds a remarkable sense of proportion in Acts, contrary to the prevailing view of his day. The plan of the author is to concentrate on important events; those events he lays stress on are the ones that are important in the life and ministry of Paul. On the other hand,

> Where the author passes rapidly over a period or journey, we shall find reason to believe that it was marked by no striking feature and no new foundation.... Our hypothesis is that Luke's silence about an incident or person should always be investigated as a piece of evidence, on the principle that he had some reason for his silence....[31]

If this be admitted, then he would certainly not have omitted (or made only slight reference to) the account of the foundation of the Galatian churches which are so important to Paul. If the author of Acts has failed to include such an important aspect of the ministry of Paul, Ramsay argued, then we must change our opinion of him as a first-rate historian and admit that Acts and the letters of Paul cannot be harmonized and that the latter are to be preferred over the former.[32] However, if the churches in the regions of Lycaonia and Phrygia (Lystra, Derbe, Inconium, and Pisidian Antioch) be equated with the churches addressed

---

29 The author of Acts, on the other hand, follows the common Greek usage and uses regional terms.
30 SPT, p. 18.
31 SPT, p. 19.
32 This is exactly the approach John Knox has taken in his *Chapters in a Life of Paul* (New York and Nashville: Abingdon Press, 1950).

in Paul's Epistle to the Galatians, then the two books fit together perfectly in this regard.

According to Ramsay, τὴν Φρυγίαν καὶ Γαλατικὴν χώραν (Acts 16:6) refers to "the Phrygio-Galatic region," i.e. that part of the Roman province of Galatia known as Phrygia. The similar expression in Acts 18:23 (τὴν Γαλατικὴν χώραν καὶ Φρυγίαν) was taken to mean the Galatic region of Lycaonia (as distinct from that part of Lycaonia which did not lie within the province of Galatia) and the Phrygian region; the first term would refer to the cities of Derbe and Lystra, and the second, to Iconium and Pisidian Antioch.[33]

Other incidental factors contribute to the acceptance of the South Galatian view. According to Paul's letter his first visit to the Galatians was occasioned by a physical illness (Gal. 4:13), the implication being that he had come there to convalesce. It would be extremely unlikely that he would have gone to the North Galatian district, an area far off the beaten track and necessitating a very difficult journey. On the other hand, Ramsay knew from personal experience that it would be quite natural for a person who had contracted malarial fever in the hot lowlands of Pamphylia to journey to the higher ground of the interior to obtain relief.[34] This would go hand in hand with his arrival at Pisidian Antioch in Acts 13. Again, it is unlikely that the Juda-izers, who dogged Paul's steps, would have been active in the out-of-the-way district of North Galatia; the more accessible southern region is a better setting for their activity. Moreover, Paul makes reference in 1 Corinthians 16:1 to the fact that the churches of Galatia are to share in the collection for the Jerusalem church, and we find two members of the South Galatian churches — Gaius of Derbe[35] and Timothy of Lystra (Acts 20:4) — and no representative from North Galatia accompanying Paul to Jeru-salem, presumably with the collection.[36] Incidental details in the epistle such as the reception of the apostle by the Galatians as "a messenger [angel] of God" (Gal. 4:14; cf. incident at Lystra in Acts 14:12) and the reference to "the marks of the Lord Jesus" (Gal. 4:17; cf. the stoning in Acts 14:19) could also be taken as pointing in the direction of South Galatian recipients of the

---

33 Ramsay, "Galatia (Region of)," HDB, 2:90-91. Cf. Bruce, Acts pp. 309-310, 350.
34 SPT, pp. 92-93. Ramsay goes on to argue for the novel idea that Paul's "thorn in the flesh" (2 Cor. 12:7) was a species of chronic malarial fever. SPT, pp. 94-97.
35 The Western Text reads Doberus, which would be in Macedonia.
36 It might be suggested that there is no mention made of delegates from Corinth or Philippi. However, a good case can be made that Titus although not mentioned in Acts, represented the Corinthian church (1 Cor. 16:3; 2 Cor. 8:16-24) and that Luke was a dele-gate from Philippi. Cf. Donald Guthrie, New Testament Introduction: The Pauline Epistles (London: Tyndale Press, 1961), p. 78. Ramsay suggested that the reason Titus is not mentioned in Acts lies in the fact that he was a relative of Luke. SPT, p. 390.

letter. Finally, there is the fact that Barnabas is mentioned in Galatians 2:1 as a person well known to the readers; yet he was only on Paul's first missionary journey (i.e. to the Southern Galatian cities) and could not have visited the North Galatian area. None of these factors in and of itself demonstrates the South Galatian hypothesis. Yet the cumulative force of the evidence seems to demand the probability of this view. At least, it convinced Ramsay, and his arguments have impressed a surprising number of scholars; e.g. E. D. Burton,[37] G. S. Duncan,[38] E. J. Goodspeed,[39] W. Michaelis,[40] F. F. Bruce,[41] C. S. C. Williams,[42] H. N. Ridderbos,[43] Jack Finegan,[44] E. M. Blaiklock,[45] and Donald Guthrie.[46] Ramsay's later conclusion that an early date for Galatians provides a more satisfactory exegesis of the letter gives even more weight to the theory.[47]

But, we may ask, why was this interpretation lost for so many centuries and recovered only in the nineteenth century? The answer is clear.

> It was lost because, during the second century, the term Galatia ceased to bear the sense which it had to a Roman in the first century. The whole of central and southern Lycaonia was, before the middle of the second century, separated from Galatia, and formed into a province Lycaonia, which was united with Isauria and Cilicia under the title of "the three Eparchies," and put under the command of a governor of the highest rank. From this time onwards the true sense of the term Galatia in St. Paul's time was lost....[48]

Thus the South Galatian theory becomes a helpful ally in the defense of the trustworthiness of Acts and its setting in the first century.

Ramsay never submitted the Gospel of Luke to the same thorough study that he did Acts. However, he cannot be criticized too harshly for this because this was really outside the realm of

---

37 *A Critical and Exegetical Commentary on the Epistle to the Galatians* (Edinburgh: T. and T. Clark, 1921), pp. xvii-xliv.
38 *The Epistle of Paul to the Galatians* (London: Hodder and Stoughton, 1934), pp. xviii-xxi.
39 *An Introduction to the New Testament* (Chicago: University of Chicago Press, 1937), pp. 34-38.
40 *Einleitung in das Neue Testament* (Bern: Beg-Verlag, 1946), pp. 181-187.
41 *Acts*, p. 38.
42 *A Commentary on the Acts of the Apostles* (London: Adam and Charles Black, 1957), pp. 175-177.
43 *The Epistle of Paul to the Churches of Galatia*, trans. by Henry Zylstra (Grand Rapids, Mich.: Wm. B. Eerdmans Publishing Co., 1953), pp. 22-31.
44 *Light from the Ancient Past* (Princeton, N. J.: Princeton University Press, 2nd edition, 1959), pp. 340-345.
45 *The Acts of the Apostles* (London: Tyndale Press, 1959), pp. 104-111.
46 *NTI: Pauline Epistles*, pp. 72-79.
47 In his early writings (*CRE, SPT, HCG*) Ramsay dated the Epistle to the Galatians in the year 53, after Paul's second missionary journey. However, by the time he wrote *The Teaching of Paul in Terms of the Present Day* (1913) he had decided that an earlier date of 49, just prior to the Jerusalem Council, was preferable. Cf. "The Chronology of the Life of St. Paul as It Appears in 1920," introductory chapter added to the 14th edition of *SPT* (1920), p. xxxi.
48 *CRE*, p. 111.

his qualifications. He was an expert in Graeco-Roman studies and had little acquaintance with Palestinian and Semitic studies. In fact, there are times when one can observe that he has a definite lack of appreciation of things Semitic.[49] Nevertheless, he did make an attempt to study the Gospel.

In a review of *St. Paul the Traveller* a distinguished foreign scholar (Schürer?) challenged Ramsay's view of Luke's rank as a historian. "If Luke is a great historian, what would the author of this book make of Luke 2:1-3?"[50] The review need say no more. This was all the encouragement Ramsay needed to write another book.

According to his custom, Ramsay first published his ideas in *The Expositor* (April and June 1897) and expanded them into a book a year later. And so the book *Was Christ Born at Bethlehem?* came into being. This has remained one of the important studies on the historical problems involved in the second chapter of the Gospel according to Luke, although some of his conclusions would need to be modified today.[51]

Luke 2:1-5 reads,

> In those days a decree went out from Caesar Augustus that all the world should be enrolled. This was the first enrollment, when Quirinius was governor of Syria. And all went to be enrolled, each to his own city. And Joseph also went up from Galilee, from the city of Nazareth, to Judea, to the city of David, which is called Bethlehem, because he was of the house and lineage of David, to be enrolled with Mary, his betrothed, who was with child.

Against the historicity of this statement, the following points had been advanced: (1) There is no evidence for a general census of the whole Roman world in the time of Caesar Augustus. (2) Even if there were such a census, it would not have been held in Palestine during the reign of Herod the Great. (3) Even if there had been a census made in Palestine, there would have been no necessity for Joseph and Mary to travel to Bethlehem. (4) No such census was ever held in Judea until A.D. 6-7; Josephus regards the census at that time as an innovation which caused a Jewish rebellion on that account. (5) A census held under Quirinius could not be held while Herod was king, for he was not the governor of Syria until a decade after Herod's death.[52]

Taking his cue from the newly discovered papyri that indicated there was a regular census in Egypt every fourteen years,

49 Cf. *SPT*, pp. 368-370; *LSC*, p. 72.
50 *BRD*, p. 223.
51 For a discussion of the problems involved, see Jack Finegan, *Handbook of Biblical Chronology* (Princeton, N. J.: Princeton University Press, 1964), pp. 234-238; Lily Ross Taylor, "Quirinius and the Census of Judea," *American Journal of Philology*, 54 (1933): 120-133; A. N. Sherwin-White, *Roman Society and Roman Law in the New Testament* (London: Oxford University Press, 1963), pp. 162-171.
52 *WCB*, pp. 102-110.

Ramsay demonstrated that there could well have been a census in Judea previous to the one mentioned in Acts 5:27. Evidence that Ramsay included in his study and more recent evidence has led many scholars to conclude — contrary to the opposition — that an earlier enrollment, as described by Luke,

(a) may have taken place in the reign of Herod the Great, (b) may have involved the return of everyone to his family home, (c) may have formed part of an empire-wide census, and (d) may have been held during a previous governorship of Quirinius over Syria.[53]

The problem of Quirinius is a thorny one, and there is still no definite proof that he served as governor during the time of the census mentioned in Luke 2. However, we cannot assume that Luke is in error in regard to this detail when he has been demonstrated to be so carefully accurate elsewhere. A recent scholar who has devoted a great deal of study to the problem of New Testament chronology concludes his discussion of this problem with a suggestion:

The question remains whether, at some time in the latter years of Herod, Quirinius might have been connected with such a census in Palestine. Since Quirinius was a high Roman official with important assignments in the East, and since at least by 6 B.C. the Homanadensian War was probably under control, this does not appear unlikely. Tertullian says in fact that the census at the time of the birth of Jesus was "taken in Judea by Sentius Saturninus." According to the list of governors of Syria this would mean sometime in the years 9-6 B.C. No reason is evident why Quirinius could not have been associated with Saturninus in such a project. In view of the sequence of known events in his career a likely time might have been in 6 or 5 B.C. That Quirinius actually took this census is still only concretely affirmed by Lk. 2:2; under the circumstances as we have reconstructed them the affirmation is not unlikely.[54]

Several other interesting aspects of Luke's Gospel are discussed in *Was Christ Born at Bethlehem?* Ramsay's study begins with an exegesis of Luke's statement of the purpose in the first four verses of his first book. He concludes (1) that Luke claims to have access to authorities of the first rank, (2) that he had made a careful and thorough personal investigation of the origin and developments of the events he is about to narrate, (3) that his intention is to give a comprehensive narrative of the events from the first to the last, and (4) that he makes an emphatic claim that his account is trustworthy and certain.[55] Ramsay goes on to observe a number of details which point to the conclusion that the author's point of view is that of a Greek provincial and that

53 Bruce, *The New Testament Documents: Are They Reliable?* (Fifth edition, London: Inter-Varsity Fellowship, 1961), p. 86.
54 Finegan, *Chronology*, pp. 237-238.
55 *WCB*, pp. 3-22.

he is writing with a single Roman or a Roman circle of readers in view.[56] Ramsay's discussion of the story with the birth of Christ may lack depth, but his theory that the narrative bears the mark of a private family tradition which would likely have been gained from a personal conversation with Mary, or someone close to her, is an attractive one.[57]

56 WCB, pp. 49-72.
57 WCB, pp. 73-91.

III

PAUL THE MISSIONARY STATESMAN

It is as an interpreter of the New Testament, rather than as an apologist, that Sir William Ramsay is at his best. When he turns the searchlight of his vast knowledge concerning the life of the first-century Roman Empire upon the Book of Acts, the epistles of Paul, or some other part of the early Christian literature, the New Testament at once comes to life for the student. When all is said and done, Ramsay's major contribution to New Testament scholarship probably lies in this area.

When he begins to study the life of the Apostle Paul, the student must first determine the value and the relationship between his basic sources. The sources that present themselves to the student are two: the Acts of the Apostles and the group of letters identified as having been written by Paul himself. How, then, are these two sources related? And what contribution do they make to the reconstruction of the life and work of Paul? Are both to be accepted as equal authorities? Furthermore, are all the letters purported to have been written by Paul really his? The answers given to these questions will determine one's approach to the study of the life of Paul; they will also to some degree determine the resulting picture of the man Paul.

The approach of John Knox in his *Chapters in a Life of Paul* is typical of a certain group of New Testament scholars.[1] In breaking ground for the construction of an outline of the life of Paul, Knox maintains, first of all, that Acts must be regarded as secondary and that Paul's letters are to be regarded as the pri-

---

1 Cf. Martin Dibelius, *Paul*, edited and completed by Werner Georg Kümmel, trans. by Frank Clarke (London: Longmans, Green, and Co., 1953), pp. 1-14.

mary source materials. Now everyone would agree with this statement in its abstract form. However, in the hands of Knox and
other critics this thesis becomes a tool to demonstrate the necessary contradiction between the two sources; it almost seems as
though the author of Acts is pre-judged in the matter. The result
is that the biographical data contained in the letters of Paul are
pitted over against the material contained in the Acts. In addition, Knox and other scholars assume that the letters of Paul to
Timothy and Titus, known as the Pastorals, and the so-called
Epistle to the Ephesians (perhaps 2 Thessalonians and Colossians
as well) are pseudonymous and, therefore, cannot be considered
as source materials.

The view expressed here is not a new one; it was current in the
time of Ramsay, although it may have been stated in a slightly
different form. Through a thorough comparison of the Acts with
the letters of Paul, Ramsay became convinced that the opposite
of this was true. If Luke was the first-rate historian that Ramsay
had judged him to be, and if he was the personal friend and dis-
ciple of Paul, then there must be a basic agreement between the
biographical data concerning Paul in Acts and the autobiograph-
ical material of his letters. Otherwise, we would have to change
our opinion concerning his character as a historian. Ramsay
argues forcefully:

> We must face the facts boldly. If Luke wrote Acts, his narrative *must*
> agree in a striking and convincing way with Paul's: they *must* confirm,
> explain and complete one another. This is not a case of two common-
> place, imperfectly educated, and not very observant witnesses who give
> divergent accounts of certain incidents which they saw without paying
> much attention to them. We have here two men of high education, one
> writing a formal history, the other speaking under every obligation of
> honour and conscience to be careful in his words: the subjects they
> speak of were of the most overpowering interest to both: their points of
> view must be very similar, for they are personal friends, and one was
> the teacher of the other, and naturally had moulded to some extent his
> mind during long companionship. If ever there was a case in which
> striking agreement was demanded by historical criticism between two
> classes of documents, it is between the writings of Paul and Luke.[2]

The Paul portrayed by Luke the historian was

> the centre of interest wherever he went, dominating all by his personal-
> ity, heralded before he came, alike in Thessalonica and in Rome, the
> man that has "turned the world upside down," the storm-centre of
> society, from whom originates revolution wherever he goes, educated in
> his thoughts and polished in his tone of courtesy, yet fiery and vehement
> in his temper, versatile and adaptable so that he moves at his ease in
> every class of society, the Socratic dialectician in the Athenian market-
> place, the philosophic rhetorician in the Ephesian School of Tyrannus,

---

2 *SPT*, pp. 14-15; cf. Bruce, *Acts*, pp. 34-40.

conversing in a tone of courteous respect with Kings and great Roman officials, "standing" before an Emperor, giving wise advice at a hasty council on a ship in the season of danger, cheering a dejected crew to make one more effort for life, reminding Roman soldiers of their duty and Roman colonial magistrates of their error in trampling on Roman law, making a great trade corporation anxious about the future of its business and a small firm of slave-owners despondent about its income, the friend of the leading men in the province of Asia, to whom a wealthy Roman procurator with a queen as his mistress looked expecting to receive bribes: where Paul is, all eyes and many hearts are attracted, while the vulgar and the mob and the Jews, the magians [sic] and the soothsayers, hate and fear him.[3]

That this picture painted by Luke of the great apostle is a true one is the presupposition of all but Ramsay's earliest discussions of the life and work of Paul. Ramsay argued that Acts and the letters of Paul can be demonstrated to complement — rather than contradict — each other. If either of them is neglected, the portrait of Paul is only partial; if they are put side by side, the information contained in both fits together, and the result is Paul in the round. In short, both Acts and the Pauline corpus are found to illuminate each other. And what about the disputed letters of Paul? Ramsay answered that the versatile man presented to us by Luke was certainly capable of writing in many veins; he, therefore, concluded that all thirteen of Paul's letters are genuine and can be treated as primary sources for a life of Paul.

In the writings of Ramsay it is Paul the man who is brought to life before the eyes of the student. The character of Paul takes on flesh and blood as the world in which he moved and the forces that molded his thoughts are unveiled for the reader, and when small — almost overlooked — details from the text of Acts or from one of his letters are breathed upon by Ramsay. W. F. Howard gives this testimony concerning *St. Paul the Traveller and the Roman Citizen*:

Many who have devoted their lives to New Testament studies would say that their first eager interest in the Pauline writings was aroused by Lightfoot's *Galatians*, but their enthusiasm for Paul the man was kindled by this never-to-be-forgotten book of Ramsay's.[4]

Not only does Paul come to life, but also his missionary associates, Christian friends, enemies, and people met along the way — Barnabas, John Mark, Silas, Luke, Apollos, Priscilla and Aquila, Timothy, Elymas the magician, Demetrius the silversmith, Sergius Paulus, Gallio, Felix, Festus, and a whole host of others. The cities visited by the Apostles also become to the student

3 *TP*, pp. vi-vii.
4 *Romance*, pp. 147-148.

more than mere names on a map or on a page in his notebook; each one — Tarsus, Syrian Antioch, Paphos, Pisidian Antioch, Iconium, Lystra, Derbe, Philippi, Thessalonica, Beroea, Athens, Corinth, Ephesus — has its own distinctive personality and makes its own contribution toward a better understanding of Paul's world and work.

As has already been indicated, Ramsay brings Paul and his companions to life by expertly filling in the background of the Acts and the Pauline letters by describing the world in which he moved. This is accomplished mainly by two works: *St. Paul the Traveller and the Roman Citizen* and *The Cities of St. Paul.* The first of these is a study of the text of the Book of Acts, especially the latter part of the book which deals with the life and missionary travels of Paul, from the viewpoint of its setting in the history and culture of the Roman Empire. The second, published twelve years later, surveys the history of five Pauline cities[5] — Tarsus, Pisidian Antioch, Iconium, Derbe, and Lystra — and seeks to determine what special aspects of the life of each of these cities has a bearing on Paul's life and thought. In both of these books he brings many interesting facts gained from a study of the cultural history of the eastern Roman provinces to bear upon the interpretation of the New Testament.

Some of the suggestions he makes regarding the background or the interpretation of a given passage of Scripture seem to be the product of a fantastic imagination. However, before one is quick to criticize Ramsay in this regard, he should be careful to ponder his method. His method in biblical study was the same as his geographical method. It was his custom to make an educated guess regarding the location of a certain city after he had thoroughly studied all the data available; then he proceeded to test his hypothesis. In this work a vivid imagination was a great asset. He was quite often wrong in his hypothesis, but he was more often correct. At any rate, his hypothesis concerning any given situation was something solid to work with, something he could put to the test to see whether it was after all true. So it is in his study of the New Testament. Many of his suggestions regarding the interpretation of a given passage of Scripture are merely educated guesses concerning what might possibly be the

---

5 The essay on Tarsus (CSP, pp. 85-244) is still the most substantial survey of the history of Tarsus. All of these articles are still valuable, for very little work has been done in regard to these cities since the days of Ramsay. Ramsay's suggestion for the location of Derbe must be altered, however, in view of its location in 1956 by M. Ballance; it was found to be more than thirty miles distant from the mound suggested by Ramsay. Cf. H. Ballance, *Anatolian Studies,* 7 (1957): 147-151.

background of the passage or what might possibly be the answer to some thorny problem that had been eluding interpreters for years. If his hypothesis did not turn out to fit all the facts of the case, Ramsay himself would be the first to reject it upon the basis of further consideration. In addition to his change of mind regarding the date of Galatians, which was mentioned in chapter two, an apt illustration is his interpretation of 1 Corinthians 2. In *St. Paul the Traveller* he regarded Paul's determination "to know nothing except Jesus Christ and him crucified" (1 Cor. 2:2) at Corinth as a new departure in his approach arising out of the disappointment and disillusionment experienced at Athens, where he attempted to present his doctrine in a form suited to Greek philosophy.[6] Later in *The Teaching of Paul in Terms of the Present Day*, Ramsay acknowledged that he had failed to take into consideration Paul's adaptation of the gospel message to different classes of hearers — tradesmen at Corinth and philosophers at Athens — and that his address before the Areopagus should be considered as typical of his method of speaking to educated Hellenic audiences.[7] However, the student should be careful before he rejects any of Ramsay's suggestions as too fantastic. The present writer can testify that he has more than once at first glance judged some interpretation of Ramsay's as fanciful only to come back to it after further reflection!

The Paul of the New Testament is a citizen of three worlds: the Roman, the Greek, and the Hebrew. Each of these worlds molded him; each influenced his personality and left its mark upon his thought. Paul wrote in Galatians 1:15-16 that God had set him apart before his birth and had called him to preach the gospel among the Gentiles. Here Paul expresses, according to Ramsay, a consciousness that his conversion and calling were the consummation of a process of selection and preparation that began a long time before his birth. This means that

> the family, the surroundings, and the education of Paul had been selected with the perfection of a Divine purpose to make him fit to be what he was designed to be, the Apostle of the Gentiles. There was one nation, one family and one city, out of which the Apostle must arise. The nation was the Jewish; but the family was not Palestinian, it was Tarsian. Only "a Hebrew sprung from Hebrews" could be the Apostle of the perfected Judaic faith; but he must be born and brought up in childhood among the Gentiles, a citizen of a Gentile city, and a member of that conquering aristocracy of Romans which ruled all the cities of the Mediterranean world. The Apostle to the Gentiles must be a Jew, a Tarsian citizen, and at the same time a Roman.[8]

---

6 Pp. 145, 252-253.
7 Pp. 109-112.
8 CSP, p. 87.

Each one of these aspects of Paul's background must be taken into consideration by the student of Paul. To neglect one of them is to fail to understand him fully. Paul was, in the first place, a Jew — "A Hebrew born of Hebrews," as he wrote to the Philippian church (Phil. 3:5). This aspect of his personality was of greatest significance in shaping the man Paul and must be carefully noted in any discussion of his life and work.[9] This heritage as a Jew produced in him his basic religious convictions and gave him an open door for his message throughout the Roman world in the synagogues of the Dispersion.

However, Paul was not a narrow Jew ignorant of and hostile to Hellenic education. He was, indeed, a good Jew, but he was far more than a Jew. He was also a patriotic citizen of Tarsus and a loyal Roman. When he speaks of himself as a Pharisee (Acts 23:6; Phil. 3:5), he identifies himself with the highest ideals of Pharisaism, not with their extreme separatism and their anti-Greek and anti-Roman feelings. Paul was educated by his parents to appreciate the best of each of the worlds in which he found himself; he assimilated the good and rejected the rest.

In the second place, Paul was from Tarsus and "a citizen of no mean city" (Acts 21:39). He was not merely born there, but he had the rights of a citizen there. It is probable that his family was planted in Tarsus about 171 B.C. by Antiochus IV along with other Jews and that they were given full rights as citizens of the city.[10] According to Ramsay, Tarsus was the ideal city to produce a man like Paul, for it was the one city that was more successful than any other in uniting the oriental and the occidental elements in its society.[11]

> It was the one city which was suited by its equipoise between the Asiatic and the Western spirit to mold the character of the great Hellenist Jew; and . . . it nourished in him a strong sense of loyalty and patriotism as the "citizen of no mean city."[12]

In the uniting of the two spirits in Tarsus, the oriental seemed to dominate. Ramsay brings this fact to bear upon the interpretation of Paul's prescription concerning the veiling of women in 1 Corinthians 11:3-16. His remarks are worth quoting in detail.

> We may notice in passing how strong an effect was produced on the

---

9 It must be admitted that Ramsay, because of his reaction against those scholars who tended to interpret Paul too narrowly within the confines of Palestinian Judaism and because of his lack of equipment in things Judaic, tended to over-emphasize the Graeco-Roman background of Paul. His discussion of Paul ought to be balanced by the insights of W. D. Davies, *Paul and Rabbinic Judaism* (London: S. P. C. K., 1948) and W. C. Van Unnik, *Tarsus or Jerusalem, the City of Paul's Youth?*, trans. by G. Ogg (London: Epworth Press, 1962).
10 *CSP*, pp. 174-180.
11 *CSP*, pp. 88-89.
12 *CSP*, p. 235.

mind of St. Paul by his Tarsian experience.... The Apostle prescribes
to the Corinthians a very strict rule about the veiling of women (I Cor.
xi 3-16). Whereas men are to have their heads uncovered in Church, it is
disgraceful for women to be unveiled there. Now it would be quite possible that a Greek or a Roman should reach this opinion about women's
dress and conduct in Church. So far as this command goes, it was quite
in accordance with the ideas of the most orderly and thoughtful among
those peoples and quite in keeping with the customs of good society.
But there is one little touch in St. Paul's sermon about women that re-
veals the man brought up amid Oriental custom. He says that "the
woman ought to have authority (ἐξουσία) upon her head." This seems
so strange to the Western mind that the words have been generally reck-
oned among the most obscure in the whole of the Pauline writings....
Most of the ancient and modern commentators say that the "authority"
which the woman wears on her head is the authority to which she is
subject — a preposterous idea which a Greek scholar would laugh at
anywhere except in the New Testament, where (as they seem to think)
Greek words may mean anything that commentators choose. Authority
or power that belongs to the wearer, such power as the magistrate pos-
sesses in virtue of his office, was meant by the Greek word ἐξουσία. . . .
The woman who has a veil on her head wears authority on her head:
that is what the Greek text says. To the European the words are unintelligible; but that is because he is a European. He must cease for a
moment to be a European and pass into the realm of life and thought
in which the words apply. Then he will understand them. To the Oriental the words are simple and clear: they describe the ordinary fact of
life....
In Oriental lands the veil is the power and the honour and dignity of
the woman. With the veil on her head, she can go anywhere in security
and profound respect. She is not seen; it is the mark of thoroughly bad
manners to observe a veiled woman in the street. She is alone. The rest
of the people around are non-existent to her, as she is to them. She
is supreme in the crowd. She passes at her own free choice, and a space
must be left for her....
But without the veil the woman is a thing of nought, whom any one
may insult. The true Oriental, if uneducated in Western ways, seems to
be inclined naturally to treat with rudeness, to push and ill-treat, a
European lady in the street. A woman's authority and dignity vanish
along with the all-covering veil that she discards. That is the Oriental
view, which Paul learned in Tarsus.[13]

In the third place, Paul was a Roman citizen.[14]

That character superseded all others before the law and the general
opinion of society; and placed him amid the aristocracy of any provincial town. In the first century, when the citizenship was still jealously
guarded, the *civitas* may be taken as a proof that his family was one of
distinction and at least moderate wealth. It also implies that there was
in the surroundings amid which he grew up, a certain attitude of
friendliness to the Imperial government....[15]

---

13 CSP, pp. 202-205. But cf. F. W. Grosheide, *Commentary on the First Epistle to the Corinthians* (Grand Rapids, Mich.: Wm. B. Eerdmans, 1953), and Leon Morris, *The First Epistle of Paul to the Corinthians* (London: Tyndale Press, 1958), *loc. cit.*
14 For an excellent recent discussion of Paul's citizenship, see Sherwin-White, *Roman Society*, pp. 144-162.
15 SPT, pp. 30-31.

Paul's Roman citizenship influenced his thought and ministry in a number of ways. Besides the obvious fact that it got him out of jams on a number of occasions, it influenced his plan of making centers of Roman administration and Greek culture centers for his evangelistic activity and his vision of a world-wide church after the order of the Empire. Paul, the Roman, was a missionary statesman "animated with the instinct of administration"; he developed the conception of the church as consisting of many parts, widely separated by geography and self-governing units, yet each part the perfect ideal of the whole after the analogy of the Roman view that "every group of Roman citizens meeting together in a body *(conventus Civium Romanorum)* in any part of the vast Empire formed a part of the great conception 'Rome,' and that such a group was not an intelligible idea, except as a piece of the great unity.[16]

In a remarkable essay published in *The Contemporary Review* in 1901 and republished five years later as a chapter in *Pauline and Other Studies*,[17] Ramsay discussed in detail Paul's Roman point of view and his imperial ideals. He pointed out that the Roman policy of the first century of our era aimed at the amalgamation of the various races and nations into a unity, with Rome at the center. Old national lines of separation were deliberately obliterated. This imperial ideal was the great fact of the age in which Paul lived and had a profound influence on his life and thought.

As Paul the young, devout Jew grew up he would have been impressed with two facts: "the lofty, stern purity of the true Judaism among the pagan world, and the danger that the Jews might slip back towards the pagan level."[18] Only one remedy for the situation presented itself to him: "Judaism in the midst of Roman society must assimilate that society and raise it to a higher level, or it must perish."[19] Either Judaism must conquer the Empire, or it must be conquered by it; it must be a power to raise Graeco-Roman society to its own level, or it must sink to the level of that society. There were no other alternatives open to him. His goal from his youth must have been to see the religion of his race become the religion of the Empire. However, it was not until after his conversion to Jesus as the Messiah that he saw the possibility of making this goal a reality.

As a Christian Paul slowly came to realize that God no longer

---

16 *SPT*, p. 125; cf. pp. 135-140.
17 Pp. 49-100.
18 *POS*, pp. 65-66.
19 *POS*, p. 66.

confined His work primarily to the Jewish people, but that Christ had made both Jew and Gentile one and that the Word of God was to go out to all men. This he came to realize early in his ministry as an apostle, but it was not until his second missionary journey, when he fixed his eyes on Ephesus, that we begin to see his deliberate strategy for the conquest of the Empire. From this moment forward it becomes obvious to all that his aim is co-extensive with the Empire: he thinks in terms of Roman provinces; he organizes his scattered congregations in the East into a unity as extensive as the Imperial organization; and he begins to make plans to visit Rome on his way to Spain, the extreme limit of the Western Roman Empire.

It is strange that Ramsay only made incidental reference to Paul's scheme of a general contribution to be collected among the churches of Galatia, Asia, Macedonia, and Achaia for the poor of the Jerusalem church, although this plan fits in perfectly with his observations concerning the Apostle's imperialistic ideals. In his discussion of Paul's background and relation to the Roman, Greek, and Hebrew worlds, he also failed to dilate upon the Pauline principle of becoming "all things to all men" as stated in 1 Corinthians 9.

In addition to his discussion of the life and work of Paul in the two books mentioned above and in his commentary on Galatians, which was noted in chapter two, Ramsay produced several other works that are concerned primarily with Paul. Two more historical commentaries were written for *The Expositor*, but they were never published separately. These were "A Historical Commentary on the Epistles to the Corinthians," published during the first eleven months of 1900, and "A Historical Commentary on the Epistles of Timothy," published over the period 1909-1911. In 1909 he wrote a series of fifty-two articles for *The Sunday School Times* (Philadelphia) on the Acts of the Apostles; these were published a year later under the title, *Pictures of the Apostolic Church*. Another work on Paul, *The Teaching of Paul in Terms of the Present Day*, was published in 1913; although it contains some significant remarks regarding the relationship of Paul to the mystery religions,[20] it falls far below the general standard of his other work. In fact, the general observation may be made that his later work in the biblical area — especially when he is concerned with exegesis and theology, rather than historical backgrounds — is much below the high quality of his earlier work. Ramsay had gained a reputation as a writer, and there was

---

20 *TP*, pp. 283-305.

a market for his books. Possibly due to the urging of his publisher, every year or so a group of his essays were gathered together without much rhyme or reason — and without an index! — and were thrust into the hands of an eager reading public. *Luke the Physician and Other Studies in the History of Religion* and *Pauline and Other Studies* are the most notable examples of this sort of action.

Ramsay commented on so many incidents in the life of Paul and so many different passages of the New Testament that it would be impossible even to list his most significant comments. The reader's best introduction to Ramsay as an expositor would be to read his comments on various subjects and biblical passages of special interest to him. As an aid in this connection, the reader is referred to the indexes of select subjects and biblical references appended to this book.

IV

THE SEVEN CHURCHES OF ASIA

A basic principle in the interpretation of the Bible is that one must first ask what a given Scripture was intended to mean to the people for whom it was originally written; only then is the interpreter free to ask what meaning it has for Christians today.

Failure to ask this primary question and to investigate the historical setting of Scripture have prevented many Christians from coming to a correct understanding of some parts of the Bible. Nowhere is this more true than in respect to the last book in the Bible. Here there has been a singular lack of appreciation for the historical background of the book; the book has been interpreted as if it were primarily written for the day in which the expositor lives (which is usually thought to be the end time), rather than in terms of what it meant to the first-century Christians of the Roman province of Asia for whom it was originally written. This has resulted in all sorts of grotesque and fantastic conclusions of which the author of the Revelation and its early recipients never would have dreamed.

In all his writings Ramsay has underlined the importance of the historical setting of the various books of the New Testament for their interpretation. He has done this in regard to the Revelation in his work on *The Letters to the Seven Churches of Asia and Their Place in the Plan of the Apocalypse*. As with so many of his works, this one was also first published as a series of essays in *The Expositor* and later in book form (1904). *The Letters to the Seven Churches* is not generally so well known as Ramsay's other books, but it is most certainly one of his more important ones. It is still the only work of a scholarly nature that has been devoted to a historical survey of the life of these seven Asian cities as a background to the understanding of the Apocalypse.[1]

Ramsay begins his work with a series of general essays portraying the world in which these early Christian communities grew up. The second part of the book is devoted to a detailed interpretation of each of the seven letters in light of the principles laid down and the features of the historical background discussed in the earlier part of the book. The author's point of view is strongly preterist; that is, he argues that the Book of Revelation as a whole must be interpreted in terms of its historical setting in the first century of the Christian era, true to the cultural and political situation in the Roman province of Asia at that time, and as it would have been understood by the members of those seven churches who were undergoing a period of intense persecution during the reign of the Emperor Domitian (A.D. 81-96). It must be understood as having only the most general reference to the future. He boldly rejects the futuristic interpretation: "The most dangerous kind of error that can be made about the Apocalypse is to regard it as a literal statement and prediction of events."[2]

The introductory chapters of the book on letter writing and travel in the first century, especially among the early Christian communities, combine to make an important contribution to the discussion of the origin and nature of the early Christian literature.[3] A good deal has been written on the subject by men who are technical theologians and biblical scholars, but here is a survey of the matter by a scholar who is intimately acquainted with the customs and culture of the Roman Empire in this regard.

Ramsay observes that it was easier and safer to send letters and to travel widely during the first century than ever before; in fact, it was much easier and safer in that part of the world in the first century A.D. than it was in Ramsay's day. This constant communication by letter, supplemented by travelling, was the greatest factor in binding together all the individual and independent churches into one universal church.[4] Ramsay argued that the Christian church developed a new type of letter that does not

---

1 Ethelbert Stauffer, *Christ and the Caesars* (London: SCM Press, 1955) contains much valuable background information concerning the imperial cult and the life of the Roman Empire, but it is not devoted primarily to Asia. David Magie, *Roman Rule in Asia Minor* (2 vols.; Princeton: Princeton University Press, 1950) and A. H. M. Jones, *The Cities of the Eastern Roman Provinces* (London: Oxford University Press, 1937), pp. 28-95, also contain a great deal of information, but there is no reference to its place in the interpretation of the New Testament. There is much material related to the life of the seven cities mentioned in the Apocalypse contained in these works, but it must be extracted and applied by the biblical interpreter.

2 *LSC*, p. 112.

3 *LSC*, pp. 1-34. Much of this material is also contained in Ramsay's essay on "Roads and Travel in the New Testament" in the extra volume of *HDB*.

4 *LSC*, p. 21.

really fall into the two categories identified by Adolf Deissmann.[5] The early Christian letters are not really true letters, and they are not stricty literary epistles. That is, they are not merely personal and occasional letters, intended only for the eye of the person or persons addressed; and they are not written primarily for public display. Some aspects of both categories are combined in these early Christian letters.

> These are true letters, in the sense that they spring from the heart of the writers; that they were often written in answer to a question, or called forth by some special crisis in the history of the persons addressed, so that they rise out of the actual situation in which the writer conceives the readers to be placed; ,that they express the writer's keen and living sympathy with the participation in the fortunes of the whole class addressed; that they are not affected by any thought of a wider public than the persons whom he directly addresses; in short, he empties out his heart in them. On the other hand, the letters of this class express general principles of life and conduct, religion and ethics, applicable to a wider range of circumstances than those which have called forth the special letter; and they appeal as emphatically and intimately to all Christians in all times as they did to those addressed in the first instance.[6]

Paul's letter to the Colossian church illustrates this double character. In bidding the Colossian Christians to share the letter with their Laodicean brethren, he recognized that what he had written had a wider application than just to the Colossian situation. But the letter was not composed primarily with that wider circle in view, but the critical situation at Colossae in mind. "The wider application arises out of the essential similarity of human nature in both congregations and in all mankind."[7] The situation that has arisen here is likely to arise elsewhere some other time. In this lies the newness of the early Christian letters:

> In the individual case they discover the universal principle, and state it in such a way as to reach the heart of every man similarly situated; and yet they state this, not in the way of formal exposition, but in the way of direct personal converse, written in place of spoken.[8]

Such letters are somewhat analogous to the imperial rescripts, which were strictly only replies to requests of guidance in special cases, but which were regarded as setting forth the general principles of policy that applied to the special case. Some of the letters of Paul take on the most personal quality, and the so-called Catholic Epistles tend to be more literary; yet neither group falls easily into either of Deissmann's two categories. Even though the letters to the seven churches of Asia in chapters two and three of

5 *Light from the Ancient East*, trans. by Lionel R. M. Strachan (3rd edition: New York and London: Harper and Brothers, 1927), pp. 228-230.
6 LSC, pp. 24-25.
7 LSC, p. 25.
8 LSC, p. 25.

the Revelation are part of a larger literary work and were never intended to be circulated separately, they also partake of the same dual character as the other early Christian letters. They are intensely personal, with the unique situation of each individual church in mind; yet they have a message for the whole church in the province of Asia, the church of God scattered throughout the Empire, and the Christian church of any age.

Although Ramsay recognizes that much of the symbolism of the Apocalypse is Jewish (especially in the latter part), he argues that there is a much greater influence of the Graeco-Roman world on the symbolism of the book than is generally recognized by commentators.[9] This is especially true of the letters contained in the second and third chapters, which are filled with allusions to the life and character of each individual city and the social, religious, and political situation of the province of Asia in the first century. The natural scenery, the geographical surroundings, the history, the traditions, the political life — all bear upon the imagery of the letters, and therefore, must not be neglected in the attempt to interpret any given symbol.[10]

Ramsay considers the Apostle John to be the author of the book. The book was written during his banishment to the island of Patmos during the persecution of the church under Domitian. One mark of its apostolic origin is its tone of "unhesitating and unlimited authority" which is so different from the other examples of early Christian literature written by non-apostolic authors (e.g., Clement of Rome and Ignatius).[11] Following a brief discussion of the problem of authorship, Ramsay goes on to describe various aspects of the general historical background of the book: the Flavian persecution in the province of Asia, the organization and character of the imperial religion, the character of cities of Asia as meeting places of the Greek and Asiatic spirit, the Jews in the province of Asia, and the place and influence of pagan converts to Christianity in the life of the early church. All of these discussions provide excellent materials for understanding the historical situation of these early churches; the chapters on the imperial religion[12] are important not only as background to the Apocalypse, but also as a part of the background of the life of the New Testament church in general.

---

9 Ramsay's general lack of sympathy for the Jewish aspect of the New Testament must be noted once again. *The Letters to the Seven Churches* is marred by a singular lack of appreciation of the apocalyptic form of literature. According to Ramsay, John's work achieves spiritual and literary greatness only to the degree he is able to free himself from the apocalyptic form, "which seriously fettered and impeded him by its fanciful and unreal character"! *LSC*, p. 35; cf. p. 72.
10 *LSC*, pp. 50-56.
11 *LSC*, pp. 74-81.
12 *LSC*, pp. 114-117.

The question has often been asked as to why these seven churches are the only churches of the province of Asia mentioned in the Revelation. It is certain that there were many other churches in the province, some of which were located in even more important cities than several of those included in the list. It is obvious that the number seven has symbolic importance for the author, but the question still remains as to why these particular seven churches were selected. James Moffatt confesses, "Why these particular churches were selected remains a mystery."[13] Martin Kiddle suggests that John's choice of this group of seven churches, rather than any other group of seven churches, was determined by "the representative nature of their problem, their varying degrees of success in meeting those problems, and their aptness as illustrative details in a symbolical design."[14] Ramsay views these seven churches as representative of seven groups of churches in the province of Asia.

> There are seven groups of Churches in Asia; each group is represented by one outstanding and conspicuous member: these representatives are the Seven Churches. These Seven representative Churches stand for the Church of the Province: and the Church of the Province, in its turn, stands for the entire Church of Christ.[15]

The question naturally follows, was this singling out of these seven churches made for the first time by John in the Apocalypse? Or was there already present in Asia the recognition of seven groups of churches? Ramsay argues for the latter view. Several factors point in this direction. First, there is the grouping of the three churches of the Lycus River valley together already when the Epistle to the Colossians was written. It seems that Laodicea gradually grew in prominence and became the administrative center of the group. This can be regarded as typical of the situation in other areas of the province. Secondly, there is the fact that all seven cities mentioned lie on the great circular road that bound together the most important region of the province of Asia. Ramsay took his cue from the observation of Hort in his notes on the First Epistle of Peter that the reason for the peculiar order in which the provinces are enumerated at the beginning of this letter lies in the route along which the messenger had to travel when he delivered the letter to the central cities of the various provinces;[16] he concluded that the circular route had an importance in determining the selection of the representative

---

13 "The Revelation of St. John the Divine," *The Expositor's Greek Testament,* W. Robertson Nicoll (ed.) Repr. Grand Rapids: Wm. B. Eerdmans, 1961), pp. 285-286, n.l.
14 *The Revelation of St. John* (London: Hodder and Stoughton, 1940), p. 7.
15 *LSC,* p. 177.
16 F. J. A. Hort, *The First Epistle of St. Peter, I. 1-II. 17* (London: Macmillan and Co., 1898), pp. 17, 157-184.

cities. This leads him to the suggestion that this was the normal order for circulating letters between the churches of the area; necessity had forced the churches to develop their own private postal system for communication with the various independent churches. The seven churches, then, would represent seven "postal districts." Copies of the book (or any occasional letter) would be delivered to each of the seven churches, from which messengers would in turn deliver copies to the various churches in their district. The result was a fast and efficient system of communication among all the churches of the province.

Ramsay contends that there is a repeated emphasis in the letters upon the continuity of history between the city and the local church; there is a strong identification of the life of the Christian community with that of the city in which it was located.[17] He goes on to find numerous allusions of the various aspects of city life and history in the letters. For example, the "crown of life" of Revelation 2:10 contains the implicit allusion to the garland of magnificent buildings with the Street of Gold, which encircled Mount Pagos, and which was poetically referred to as "the crown of Smyrna."[18] There is no doubt that Ramsay went to an extreme in finding allusions to the history and geographical setting of the cities where there were none intended; yet the basic emphasis upon the actual historical situation is sound. And his detailed studies of the individual cities are extremely illuminating to the student of the Apocalypse.

The best way to illustrate Ramsay's method is to take one of the seven cities as an example. His treatment of the letter to the church at Pergamum is representative.[19]

Pergamum is the royal city, the city of authority. Both its history and natural setting impress this picture upon the mind of the student. It is the one city of Asia that was set on a huge, rocky hill from which it dominates the whole surrounding area. (Other cities had splendid hills, but as a rule the hill was only the acropolis; the city lay beneath or around the hill.) The visitor to Pergamum cannot but be moved by the awesomeness of its location.[20] It was the seat of the ruling power of the kingdom of the Attalids before the Roman period, and it was the center of Roman rule in the province after its bequest to the Romans by Attalus III in 133 B.C. The first temple of Rome and Augustus to be built in Asia Minor was built in Pergamum *ca.* 29 B.C., and

---

17 *LSC*, p. 204.
18 *LSC*, pp. 256-259, 275.
19 *LSC*, pp. 281-315.
20 The present writer can confirm this impression by his own experience.

the city continued to be the center of the imperial cult in the province. In addition, it was the seat of the worship of Zeus, Athena, Dionysus, and Asklepios. Besides the imperial worship, the two outstanding religious features of the city in the first century A.D. were the famous altar of Zeus, high up the mountain and visible for miles around, and the Asklepieion, the center of the healing cult of the God-Serpent.

John conveys this message of the exalted Lord to the church in Pergamum:

> And to the angel of the church in Pergamum write: The words of him who has the sharp two-edged sword.
> I know where you dwell, where Satan's throne is; you hold fast my name and you did not deny my faith even in the days of Antipas my witness, my faithful one, who was killed among you, where Satan dwells. But I have a few things against you: you have some there who hold the teaching of Balaam, who taught Balak to put a stumbling block before the sons of Israel, that they might eat food sacrificed to idols and practice immorality. So you also have some who hold the teaching of the Nicolaitans. Repent then. If not, I will come to you soon and war against them with the sword of my mouth. He who has an ear, let him hear what the Spirit says to the churches. To him who conquers I will give some of the hidden manna, and I will give him a white stone, with a new name written on the stone which no one knows except him who receives it. (Rev. 2:12-17)

According to Ramsay a number of features stand out as significant in this letter in view of the character of the city. First, Christ identifies himself as the One who "has the sharp two-edged sword" (v. 12); that is, He is the One who "wears the symbol of authority, and is invested with the power of life and death,"[21] the two-edged sword being the symbol of the highest order of Roman official authority with which the proconsul of Asia was invested (*jus gladii*). The readers are reminded that Jesus Christ, rather than the Emperor and his representative, is in the final analysis the One with absolute authority.

Second, the church of Pergamum is portrayed as dwelling "where Satan's throne is" (v. 13). The reference here is primarily to the fact that Pergamum is the center of the state religion and the worship of the divine Emperor as well as the administrative capital of the province.[22] From the rest of the book it is obvious that the Christians of Asia were undergoing an intense time of persecution at the hand of the state religion. However, the reference to Satan's throne need not be limited to the Emperor cult, but may also include an allusion to the pagan activities asso-

---

21 *LSC*, p. 291.
22 Cf. 2 Thess. 2:3-4, 9-10.

ciated around the great altar of Zeus and Asklepios, all of which is abhorrent to God and to His people.

A third item illumined by the historical background is the reference to the Nicolaitans (v. 15). We do not know all the historical details we would like to know regarding this group that is mentioned in two of the seven letters, but it evidently represents an attempt at a reasonable compromise with the pagan world surrounding the church. Perhaps they argued that a pinch of incense on the altar to the Emperor was really unimportant.

The mention of the "hidden manna" (v. 17) is a touch of Judaism and possibly alludes to the tradition that the manna laid up in the Ark of the Covenant was to be revealed when Messiah comes. Here the symbol is used to indicate the heavenly food the Savior gives to sustain the believer. Finally, the reference to the "white stone" with a new name known only to the bearer written on it (v. 17) could be taken as alluding to a number of customs of the day: possibly a sort of "ticket" of admission to some special event. In contrast to a ticket or coupon for some temporary purpose, this white tessera given by the Lord is lasting and imperishable.

Whether or not one is able to follow Ramsay in all of his suggestions (and here the fact that many of these are merely suggestions must again be underlined), it must be admitted that he has set the importance of the *Sitz im Leben* of the Apocalypse in bold relief. And until someone writes a better and more up-to-date book on the subject, *The Letters to the Seven Churches* will remain a basic tool for the student in his study of the Book of Revelation.

V

POTPOURRI

Ramsay had a flair for denouncing scholars with whom he disagreed and who he felt were absolutely at odds with the facts. In this aspect of his life he belonged more to a bygone age than to the modern. When he wishes to emphasize the absurdity of his opponent's position, he heaps up sarcasm to a degree surpassed only by some of the Protestant Reformers. He confesses on more than one occasion his debt to German scholarship and his great admiration for men of the stature of Theodor Mommsen; at the same time he finds himself constantly at odds with the radical conclusions of many of the German critics. To say that he was not always unemotional in his criticism of some of the tendencies of German scholarship is an understatement. However, his judgment upon his fellow Britishers who failed to do original work and tended merely to mimic the most recent (and sometimes the not-so-recent) opinions of Continental scholarship was even more severe. In one place he apologizes for making such frequent reference to German works, but he then goes on to defend himself with the observation that some scholars will not believe anything unless it is written in German. Elsewhere he muses that some scholars seem to have imputed that same quality of inerrancy to a certain group of German critics which our grandparents reserved for the Bible!

In 1910, James Moffatt published *An Introduction to the Literature of the New Testament*[1] as the successor of his earlier work, *The Historical New Testament*.[2] His new *Introduction*

---

1 (New York: Charles Scribner's Sons, 1911).
2 (Edinburgh: T. and T. Clark, 1901).

was warmly received by the scholarly world in Britain, as were most of Moffatt's multifarious writings, even though he was much less traditional in his views than the typical British scholar. There was one notable exception to this generally friendly reception: Sir William Mitchell Ramsay! Ramsay, who was in Asia Minor at the time, exploded in a series of articles in *The Expositor* which should never have been written — certainly not in the tone in which they were written. These essays were published in book form in 1911 as *The First Christian Century: Notes on Dr. Moffatt's Introduction to the Literature of the New Testament,* and so the greatest blemish to Ramsay's reputation as a scholar was immortalized.

Ramsay said that he could at least pardon the viewpoint of the earlier work as the attempt of a brilliant — but inexperienced — "young scholar," but to be guilty of putting the same general ideas into print ten years later was unforgivable. He had hoped that Moffatt's later work would have shown a greater maturity, but he was keenly disappointed. Several quotations illustrate the tone of his review. "I can detect no broadening of the outlook, no deepening of the sympathy, little sign of growing independence of thought. The book is antiquated, as if it belonged to the nineteenth century."[3] "To put my opinion in a sentence, I should say that the author never reaches the historical point of view; he never shows any comprehension of the way in which great events work themselves out."[4] The work "savours too much of flippant journalism"[5]; it is "indicative of the literary rather than the historical temperament."[6] And so on.

Rather than give a detailed and thoroughly scholarly critique of Moffatt's work, Ramsay was content to make a few general criticisms and a few more incidental criticisms. The result was inconclusive, and Ramsay was the injured one rather than Moffatt. Even the conservative scholar, James Denney, felt compelled to comment:

> I find Sir W. M. Ramsay on Moffatt too discursive and irrelevant, and even in the ordinary sense too impertinent to be very pleasant or profitable reading. What right has he to lecture Moffatt as he does? I agree with him that Moffatt is wrong about the Papias tradition, but if one may say so, he has a right to be wrong; he is a master in this business, and Ramsay has no right to talk to him as he does.[7]

Why did Ramsay vent his wrath so unmercifully upon the

3 FCC, pp. 3-4.
4 FCC, p. 9.
5 FCC, p. 11.
6 FCC, p. 15.
7 *Letters of Principal James Denney to His Family and Friends*, edited by James Moffatt (London: Hodder and Stoughton, n.d.), p. 161.

head of James Moffatt rather than others? There were many others who held similar opinions and who wrote similar works, but he did not take time out to castigate them. Perhaps it was because Moffatt was a fellow Scot, and Ramsay felt under obligation to set him straight on this account. Or perhaps it was due to Moffatt's steadfast refusal to admit the force of Ramsay's arguments for the South Galatian hypothesis. Furthermore, Moffatt's method of balancing the opinions of the critics one against the other in determining the answer to a given problem was directly contrary to Ramsay's temperament and method. In the preface to the first edition of his *Introduction,* Moffatt lists the two great commandments of research that underlie his work. First, "Thou shalt work at the sources"; and secondly, "Thou shalt acquaint thyself with work done before thee and beside thee."[8] Now, Ramsay would not quibble with these "commandments" in their abstract form, for he certainly followed them in all of his work. But it seemed to him that Moffatt had inverted the proper order and had, in reality, given very little consideration to original research. According to Ramsay, Moffatt's work was characterized by the

> perfectly confident assumption that the right way of study lies in sifting and weighing these theories [of most recent scholarship] and thus discovering in them "here a little and there a little" which is correct and valuable. . . .[9]

The result, argues Ramsay, is that Moffatt is wrong in his initial principle, and this in turn affects the whole of his work. What does the great archaeologist suggest as a prescription for Moffatt's problem?

> Dr. Moffatt must change his method radically, before he can succeed in doing what he was born to do. He ought to give up reading modern authorities for ten years, and devote that time to thinking and studying the original authorities.[10]

If he does this, he will cease to be dominated by the thought of bad historical critics and will learn to distinguish good from bad criticism!

There is no doubt that Moffatt needed some criticism and that Ramsay's basic contention regarding Moffatt's heavy reliance upon the bulk of "modern scholarship" rather than original sources was correct. Yet *The First Christian Century* remains primarily a negative example of the would-be scholar; it is an illustration of the type of book a scholar should *not* write, or

---

8 *Introduction,* p. viii.
9 FCC, p. 4.
10 FCC, p. 199.

how *not* to win supporters for one's opinions and influence the
world of New Testament scholarship.

Some may accuse Ramsay of being too independent, but no
one is able to say that he lacked originality. This was his great
strength, as it was sometimes, alas, his weakness. Few have followed him in his suggestions regarding the First Epistle of Peter[11]
and the Epistle to the Hebrews,[12] but his views concerning both
illustrate his freedom to depart from tradition and to follow
truth wherever it may lead.

The First Epistle of Peter was the one book in the New Testament that he felt did not fit the traditionally assigned authorship
and date. He agreed with many other scholars that the picture of
the persecution of the church in Asia Minor points to a date
after the death of the Apostle Peter, which was thought to have
occurred in the seventh decade of the first century. Stimulated
by a conversation with Professor Hort, he began to consider the
possibility that the tradition concerning Peter's martyrdom was
wrong and that he did not die until a later period. He then concluded that 1 Peter was written about A.D. 75 or later by the
Apostle, whose ministry was longer than traditionally thought.[13]

His views concerning the date and authorship of the Epistle to
the Hebrews were (1) that it was written in April or May, A.D.
59, towards the end of the governorship of Felix; (2) that it
treats topics that had been frequently discussed between Paul and
the leading brethren of the church at Caesarea during his im-
prisonment there; (3) that it was really a letter from the church
in Caesarea to the Jewish party of the church in Jerusalem, represented in the writing by Philip the evangelist (Acts 21:8) ; and
(4) that the plan of writing such a letter was discussed before-
hand with Paul, the letter was submitted to him for approval,
and the last few verses were actually appended by him.[14] This
ingenious hypothesis would solve a number of the problems regarding the nature of the letter, but it would leave others unsolved and even add a few of its own. It is only mentioned as an
example of the freedom Ramsay had in his approach to the
various problems that confront New Testament scholars.

Ramsay wrote widely and at great length. His published books
contain more than eight thousand pages (rivaling F. C. Baur in
volume!) . This does not include the great mass of essays Ramsay
published in various scholarly journals and in the more popular

---

11 *CRE*, pp. 279-295.
12 *LP*, pp. 301-328.
13 *POS*, pp. 268-270.
14 *LP*, p. 304.

magazines, and the extensive articles in Hastings' *Dictionary of the Bible*. His range of interests included subjects outside the realms of Graeco-Roman studies, New Testament criticism, and the history of the early church, although the greater part of his life was devoted to these. The breadth of his concern is marked by the fact that his writings include two fair-sized volumes on modern Turkey,[15] and an essay on the idealism and dedication of the founders of an American college,[16] and a published lecture in the area of modern political science.[17] In addition, he wrote a plethora of articles over the years on the place of Turkey in international politics.

But the real heart of Sir William Ramsay is laid bare in a small book on Jesus and in a sermon preached before the students of the Moody Bible Institute in Chicago. *The Education of Christ: Hill-side Reveries,* published in 1902, is a delight to read. It is by no means a technical discussion of the life and teachings of Jesus; it is rather "the dream of a student's life,"[18] meditations of a mystical scholar (or a scholarly mystic) on the identity of the real Jesus and His significance for the history of the world. His comments on the importance of geography, especially mountains (the Temptation, the choosing of the Twelve, the Sermon on the Mount, the Transfiguration, the Mount of Olives, etc.), in the education of Jesus are extremely provocative.

This little book of less than one hundred fifty pages and his sermon on "The Cross of Christ the Center of History"[19] portray a man who is as devoted to his Master as he is to the cause of truth. Not only had the greatest of the Apostles cast his spell over Sir William, but also the great Apostle's Lord.

15 *Impressions of Turkey during Twelve Years' Wanderings* (London: 1897); Hodder and Stoughton, *The Revolution in Constantinople and Turkey: A Diary* (London: Hodder and Stoughton, 1909).

16 *The Making of a University: What We Have to Learn from Educational Ideals in America* (London: Hodder and Stoughton, 1915). An estimate of the educational work of Dr. Isaac Conrad Ketler.

17 *The Imperial Peace: An Ideal in European History* (Oxford, Clarendon Press, 1913).

18 EC, p. vii.

19 *The Christian Worker's Magazine,* 14 (Nov. 1913), pp. 140-148. Reprinted in Wilbur M. Smith, *Great Sermons on the Death of Christ* (Natick, Mass.: W. A. Wilde Co., 1965), pp. 235-241.

VI

CONCLUSION

What contributions has Sir William M. Ramsay made to the study of the New Testament? This is the question implied by the sub-title of this study. In conclusion, several of the assured results of the life and labor of the great archaeologist and scholar may be reiterated.

In his admirable study on *The Interpretation of the New Testament 1861-1961*, Bishop Stephen Neill mentions two conclusions of Ramsay which abide and should be guidelines to New Testament scholars in our day.[1] The first of these is the establishment of the accuracy and reliability of the Lukan writings. That the author of Luke-Acts is, as Ramsay discovered for himself, a first-rate historian should be the presupposition of twentieth-century New Testament scholarship. There is a growing awareness of this fact by both conservative and liberal critics, but the view is not accepted by all.[2] There is still a group of scholars — especially in Germany — who persist in ignoring the strong evidence in favor of the value of the book of Acts as a piece of historical writing. Some few even continue to hold the

---

1 Pp. 142-146.
2 Some of the scholars who have been strongly impressed in recent years by the evidence for the reliability of the Book of Acts are A. M. Hunter, *Interpreting the New Testament* (Philadelphia: Westminster Press, 1961), pp. 111-112; F. F. Bruce, *Acts*, pp. 15-18; C. S. C. Williams, *Acts*, pp. 30-31; Alfred Wikenhauser, *New Testament Introduction* (New York: Herder and Herder, 1958), pp. 329-340; E. M. Blaiklock, *Acts*, p. 89; C. F. D. Moule, *The Birth of the New Testament* (London: Adam and Charles Black, 1962), pp. 3, 109; J. A. Thompson, *The Bible and Archaeology* (Grand Rapids: Wm. B. Eerdmans, 1962), pp. 373-403; Floyd V. Filson, *Three Crucial Decades: Studies in the Book of Acts* (London: Epworth Press, 1964), pp. 5, 115; E. F. Harrison, *Introduction to the New Testament* (Grand Rapids: Wm. B. Eerdmans, 1964), pp. 229-231; and A. A. T. Ehrhardt, *The Framework of the New Testament Stories* (Manchester: Manchester University Press, 1964), pp. 64-102. To this can be added the testimony of the Roman historian, Sherwin-White, *Roman Society*, pp. 48-186.

untenable position that it was actually written in the second century.[3] Why is this?

One cannot but feel that many scholars have not taken the time and the trouble to examine the evidence. Many New Testament scholars are not aware of what has been done in the area of archaeological studies; fewer still have had first-hand experience in archaeological work. Neill observes that this is especially true of German scholars, few of whom "have any personal acquaintance with the archaeological evidence, and it is possible that they tend to underestimate its significance."[4] A. A. T. Ehrhardt makes an interesting observation. He notes that historians have generally maintained a much higher estimate of Luke as an historian than many theologians.[5] (Ramsay himself made the same observation on more than one occasion.) And it may be significant that almost every New Testament critic who has had a background in classical studies and a familiarity with archaeological work takes a very high view of Acts.

Connected with this failure to examine the archaeological evidence is the abiding influence of the ghost of F. C. Baur in Pauline and Lukan research, as both Neill[6] and Johannes Munck[7] have pointed out. Although the literary conjectures of the Tübingen school have ceased (for the most part) to be taken into account, the historical conjectures continue to be assumed as true: conclusions of development in order to be true have been transferred to a period of merely three decades.[8] So we find Martin Dibelius penning these words in 1930:

> Both Strauss and Baur made many mistakes. But in their work they made use of principles which even today give guidance in the historical investigation of the New Testament. And through the new conclusions at which they arrive, they provided the scientific study of primitive Christianity with the decisive motives for further development.[9]

One may be moved to wonder whether Dibelius has ever stopped to examine the work done by Lightfoot, Zahn, and Ramsay.[10]

There is no doubt that Ramsay's influence was harmed by the nature of some of his later work and that this has been partially the cause of his neglect. However, it is unscientific for New Testament scholars on this account to ignore the high quality and

---

3   E.g., J. C. O'Neill, *The Theology of Acts in Its Historical Setting* (London: S.P.C.K., 1961). C. K. Barrett, *Luke the Historian in Recent Study* (London: Epworth Press, 1961), pp. 62, 75, suggests a date as late as A.D. 95-115.
4   *Interpretation*, p. 145.
5   *Framework*, p. 100.
6   Pp. 58-60, 222.
7   *Paul and the Salvation of Mankind* (London: SCM Press, 1959), pp. 69-86.
8   Munck, *Paul*, p. 70.
9   "National Contributions to Biblical Science: V. The Contribution of Germany to New Testament Science," *Expository Times*, 41:536.
10   One may also be moved to wonder why, if Baur and his colleagues made use of the correct method, they came up with almost totally wrong answers.

thoroughness of his earlier work. F. F. Bruce makes this comment:

> Although in his later years Ramsay was persuaded to don the mantle of a popular apologist for the trustworthiness of the New Testament records, the judgements which he publicized in this way were judgements which he had previously formed as a scientific archaeologist and student of ancient classical history and literature.[11]

Therefore, the student of the New Testament who ignores what Ramsay had to say does so to his own peril.

A second assured result of Ramsay's work mentioned by Neill is the answer he gave to the question: Who are the Galatians? His conclusion that they were members of the churches established by Paul in the area of Derbe, Lystra, Iconium, and Pisidian Antioch (i.e., South Galatia) has been judged as correct by the majority of British and American scholars, and even by a few of the Germans.[12] J. A. Findlay claimed that "all those who know the geography of Asia Minor well are South Galatians to a man."[13] The case cannot be proved to the satisfaction of all scholars, but the strength of the evidence seems to favor the South Galatian view.

A third contribution of Ramsay comes from his repeated emphasis upon the importance of thorough historical study as foundational to the study of the New Testament. Contrary to the opinion that the attitude and actions of some conservative Christians seem to convey, the Bible did not come down from heaven bound in morocco leather and translated into Jacobean English. The message of the Bible may be an eternal one, but each of its component parts has its roots deeply imbedded in the age in which it was written and must be interpreted in terms of that age. Whatever message it has for us today should be in harmony with its original message to those who first received it as a word from God. On the other hand, contrary to the thinking of some radical critics and their disciples, it is a fact that the writers of the New Testament were not merely concerned with theology, but also with history. They all write from a certain theological point of view, but this is not to say that they are not interested in history or that what they write is historically suspect. This is especially true of the writings of Luke, as Ramsay and others have demonstrated so clearly.

Finally, we must look to the future. Ramsay was the pioneer in a great work. Who will continue what he began?

There has been no one since Ramsay who has done extensive

---

11 *The New Testament Documents*, p. 90.
12 But see Harrison, *NT Introduction*, pp. 255-266, who suggests the possibility that the North Galatian theory deserves a second look.
13 Quoted in Hunter, *Interpreting the NT*, p. 67.

work in Asia Minor and then brought the knowledge gained in this experience to the study of the New Testament. A few men have brought a profound knowledge of classical studies to the study of the book of Acts,[14] but no one who has had a first-hand acquaintance with archaeological research has yet brought this to an extensive study of the early Christian writings.

Many cities of Palestine have been excavated during the past fifty years, and the knowledge gained here and through a close study of the geography of that area of the world has greatly enhanced our understanding of the Bible. Archaeological work in Greece has been quite extensive as well, although there has not been the same diligence in the correlation of the discoveries with the data of the New Testament. However, very little work, by comparison, has been done in Asia Minor. On more than one occasion Ramsay mentions the need for thorough excavation in connection with the cities of South Galatia. This need remains to this day; only Pisidian Antioch has been studied to any great extent. Although Iconium is the site of the modern city of Konya and cannot on this account be excavated to any great degree, Lystra and the newly located site of Derbe lie waiting to be excavated by someone who has the time and the money.[15] In the area of Turkey that was formerly the Roman province of Asia, only Pergamum and Ephesus have been excavated on a large scale. Some work has been done at Smyrna over the years, and Sardis is in the process of being excavated by teams from Cornell and Harvard Universities.[16] Other cities of Asia — more than twenty-five in a hundred kilometer radius of Izmir (Smyrna) — lie exposed to the elements, ready to yield detailed knowledge concerning the life and times of the early church. The results of the work in Asia Minor and Greece that already have been obtained have yet to be closely studied by New Testament scholars and to be applied to the study of the New Testament. If and when this work is done, we may rest assured that our knowledge concerning the environment of the early church and our appreciation for the writings of the New Testament will be greatly increased. This work awaits the dedicated lives of some younger scholars who are willing to give themselves to this task.

Some years before the end of his life, Ramsay wrote a letter to

---

14 Bruce in his two commentaries that have already been mentioned; and Henry J. Cadbury, *The Book of Acts in History* (London: Adam and Charles Black, 1955).

15 During conversation in his office in the summer of 1962, the Director of Antiquities in Konya expressed a strong desire to the author for scholars to come to excavate Lystra and Derbe (and any other cities of interest in that part of Turkey).

16 Work which was set to begin at Colossae during the summer of 1965 was reportedly delayed due to lack of financial assistance.

Mr. William Ridgeway, a wealthy retired manufacturer who was an avid reader and a great admirer of his. In this letter he remarked that if he were free from other obligations, there is nothing he would rather do than to go back and rework the material concerning the book of Acts.[17] Students of the New Testament will forever regret that he was unable to do this. But even with this neglect, Sir William Mitchell Ramsay has left a great legacy to the cause of New Testament scholarship for which we can be profoundly grateful.

---

17 This information was furnished by Wilbur M. Smith, who was Mr. Ridgeway's pastor at the time.

APPENDIX

A CHRONOLOGICAL LIST OF RAMSAY'S MAJOR WORKS

The Historical Geography of Asia Minor, 1890.
The Church in the Roman Empire before A.D. 170, 1893.
St. Paul the Traveller and the Roman Citizen, 1895.
The Cities and Bishoprics of Phrygia, vol. 1, pt. 1, 1895; vol. 1,
   pt. 2, 1897.
Was Christ Born at Bethlehem?, 1898.
Articles in Hastings' *Dictionary of the Bible,* vol. 1, 1898.
   (Achaia, Adramyttium, Antioch in Pisidia, Asia, Asiarch,
   Bithynia, Cappadocia, Caria, Chios, Churches [Robbers of],
   Cilicia, Cnidus, Colossae, Corinth, Cos, Delos, Derbe, Diana,
   Ephesian, Ephesus)
Articles in Hastings' *Dictionary of the Bible,* vol. 2, 1899.
   (Galatia, Galatia [Region of], Galatians, Halicarnassus,
   Hierapolis, Iconium, Illyricum)
A Historical Commentary on St. Paul's Epistle to the Galatians,
   1899.
"A Historical Commentary on the Epistles to the Corinthians,"
   The Expositor, Jan.-Nov. 1900.
Articles in Hastings' *Dictionary of the Bible,* vol. 3, 1900.
   (Laodicea, Lasea, Lycaonia, Lycia, Lydia, Lystra, Mallus,
   Miletus, Myndus, Myra, Nicopolis, Pamphylia, Patara, Perga,
   Pergamus or Pergamum, Phaselis, Philadelphia, Phoenix,
   Phrygia, Pisidia)
The Education of Christ: Hill-Side Reveries, 1902.
Articles in Hastings' *Dictionary of the Bible,* vol. 4, 1902.
   (Pontus, Rhegium, Rhodes, Samothrace, Sardis, Smyrna,

Syracuse, Tarsus, Thracia, Thyatira, Town Clerk, Troas, Tyrannus)

Articles in Hastings' *Dictionary of the Bible,* extra vol., 1904. (Numbers, Hours, Years and Dates; Religion in Greece and Asia Minor; Roads and Travel [in NT])

Letters to the Seven Churches of Asia, 1904.

Pauline and Other Studies in Early Christian History, 1906.

Studies in the History and Art of the Eastern Provinces of the Roman Empire, written for the Quatercentenary of the University of Aberdeen by Ramsay and six of his students, 1906.

The Cities of St. Paul: Their Influence on His Life and Thought, 1907.

Luke the Physician and Other Studies in the History of Religion, 1908.

The Thousand and One Churches, with Miss Gertrude Bell, 1909.

Pictures of the Apostolic Church: Studies in the Book of Acts, 1910.

The First Christian Century: Notes on Dr. Moffatt's Introduction to the Literature of the New Testament, 1911.

"A Historical Commentary on the Epistles to Timothy," *The Expositor,* 1909-1911.

The Teaching of Paul in Terms of the Present Day, 1913.

The Bearing of Recent Discovery on the Trustworthiness of the New Testament. 1915.

Asianic Elements in Greek Civilization, 1927.

The Social Basis of Roman Power in Asia Minor, prepared for the press by J. G. C. Anderson, 1941.

APPENDIX II

AN INDEX OF SELECT SUBJECTS FROM RAMSAY'S WORKS

APPENDIX III

AN INDEX OF SCRIPTURE REFERENCES FROM RAMSAY'S WORKS

APPENDIX IV

AN INDEX OF GREEK TERMS FROM RAMSAY'S WORKS

σωτηρία, ἡ, BRD 173-177

Φρυγίαν καὶ Γαλατικὴν χώραν, τὴν, CRE 77-89, SPT 210-211

χαλάσαντες τὸ σκεῦος, SPT 329-330

χειροτονήσαντες, SPT 121-123

χώρα, ἡ, SPT 102-104, 110-113

APPENDIX V

A SUMMER JOURNEY IN ASIA MINOR[1]

by

WILLIAM M. RAMSAY

Rarely have I known such a favourable season in point of weather throughout my whole experience in Asia Minor, as that of 1905. The earlier spring and the end of winter had been extremely wet; but the fine weather began unusually early, and April and May, which generally are stormy months on the high plateau, offered a succession of bright and pleasant days, while the previous abundant rains had so clothed the mountains with green that the country was looking its best. We spent one day at Ephesus; and for the first time I was able to appreciate properly the beauty of the scenery. Perhaps it was because the hills were so green and the colours so bright, perhaps because I was only a spectator and others were charged with the entire responsibility for observing, measuring, and recording: certainly the words rose to my lips several times, "I knew that the Ephesus plain was beautiful, but I never had any idea that it was as lovely as it is now." The English excavations on the Temple of Diana have had a success, as gratifying as unexpected: the discoveries have been quite remarkable, and combine with the Cretan finds to reveal a very different character in the early Greek period from what we have been previously taught to expect. The Austrians have been working their way along a new street in the city, and every step brings up a new detail of interest. It is in Ephesus, beyond all other places, that we may expect the inscription which will give absolute certainty about the date of POLYCARP'S

1 From *The British Weekly*, July 27, 1905, pp. 377-378. (Used by permission.)

martyrdom, that much controverted point on which so many other questions turn.

As to ourselves, we had an almost unbroken series of interesting discoveries. We began by following the road to Iconium with the purpose of determining where lay the pass in which was fought the great battle of 1175 A.D., the battle which sealed the fate of the Byzantine Empire, and decided that the Turks and not the (so-called) Romans should rule Asia Minor. That same pass was the scene of an interesting episode in the march of the German Emperor BARBAROSSA, in the Third Crusade, only ten years later. The name is correctly placed on the map in Part II of my "Cities and Bishoprics of Phrygia"; I could not determine this during the journey, but since I returned and have read once more the description of the battle by NICETAS, there seems no longer any doubt. The north side of the pass was gently sloping ground, and the south side was precipitous: these and many other features suit the glen that leads east from the great double lake, Limnai, towards Pisidian Antioch. At the two ends of the pass we had the good fortune to find two extremely important inscriptions, which had escaped the many travellers who have gone along that route (including myself at the beginning of my journeys in 1882).

It is pointed out in my "Historical Commentary on Galatians," p. 211, that the vast estates which once belonged to the great Temple of Men Askainos at Pisidian Antioch must have become the personal property of the Roman Emperors when the province of Galatia was formed in 25 B.C. That has been assumed as self-evident in my later investigations in Pisidia; but it is only through the two newly discovered inscriptions that I began to realize how much is involved in this. A new page of history, and one of fascinating interest, has been opened before us. It is in recent times becoming evident that the central motive in Roman Imperial history between 200 A.D. and the triumph of the first professedly Christian Emperor, CONSTANTINE, in 312 A.D., lay in the struggle between the Christian and the Pagan element in the state. Roman Imperial history requires to be rewritten from this new point of view. The ancient historians of the Empire deliberately ignored the Christians, and intentionally wrote as if they were mere criminals occasionally brought up for trial. The modern historians have been misled into this superficial view, and wrote as if the relations between the Christians and the government before 312 A.D. consisted only in a series of occasional persecutions, until all at once this despised and ignored band of fanatics is revealed to us as the greatest power in the Empire.

Such a revolution is the result of long growth; and only a very superficial view of history would be content to set before us this sudden transformation as a reasonable account of historic evolution. The truth is that throughout the third century the critical question about every Emperor is what was his attitude to the Christians; and the test regarding almost every event is how it affected the relation of Christians and Pagans. Of the two new inscriptions which we found near the scene of the great battle, the first gives the definite proof that the country was an Imperial estate and that a series of other inscriptions also belong to the Antiochian group of estates; while the second suggests a new view as to the relation of those estates to the great question of the third century. This is a matter of wide import. The Imperial estates were a vast body of properties, and certain features were common to all of them. For years I have been studying almost alone the history of the Asian estates, just as a whole body of more distinguished scholars are now studying the African estates; and whereas not a single fact was known a few years ago about any Asian Imperial estate, the situation and character of many of them are now known, and the history of one large group of them during the years 190-240 A.D., has been traced in some detail. Now the Antiochian group of estates, a vast extent of territory, has at last been revealed; and it will take some time to piece together the scattered details regarding them; but at present I may briefly indicate their relation to the great controversy of the third century.

A group of inscriptions, some of them very long, has become known in the last twenty-four years; the first and most important was published in the "Journal of Hellenic Studies," 1883, by the present writer; others were discovered by my American friend and companion in travel, Professor Sterrett, now of Cornell. These give lists of persons, who subscribed to various hieratic purposes, and who are summed up as "Tekmoreian Guest-friends." Professor Sterrett has interpreted the word "Tekmoreian" as a topographical epithet, and marked a town Tekmorion on his map. I felt convinced that the epithet was not topographical, and sought to explain it as "the Guest-friends of the secret sign" (Tekmor, an old poetic Greek word, revived in that artificial age). Several German scholars declared against me; but one of the new inscriptions decides in my favour. One of the Guest-friends, belonging to the village Gissa near the modern city Ak-Sheher, is recorded to have twice shown (or spoken) the Tekmor; a new Greek verb, occurring nowhere else, is here employed to designate the religious act; the use of this verb demonstrates beyond a doubt that the Tekmoreian Guest-friends were those who used the Tekmor, i.e., the sign. If we try to get a clearer understanding of what this meant and how the sign was used, we are from the very nature of the case reduced to conjecture. People who employ a sign do so because they wish to avoid what is plain and open. The value of the sign lies in its being understood by the proper persons, and unintelligible to the rest of the world. It is not published; it is kept private; and accordingly future centuries can only guess what it was and how it was used. Yet the circumstances point to a certain interpretation. The inscriptions of the Guest-friends have clearly a religious bearing, therefore the Tekmor must have formed an element in some religious rite; and there is every probability that this rite must have formed part of the Mysteries. Now there is no appearance, hardly any possibility, that the Mysteries were originally of such a character as to contain a Tekmor. The very word marks this as a late Roman addition to the old ritual. This poetic, otherwise purely epic or Homeric, term could hardly be used in prose, as a word of ordinary religious speech, except in that artificial period. Elsewhere I have given some examples of the revival in that country and period, of old poetic personal names; and an inscription which we found this year at a new site where five Phrygian inscriptions gladdened us, may be quoted as a specimen of the influence of old Greek poetry; it mentions a man named PATROCLUS, son of HOMER. In publishing the first of the Tekmoreian inscriptions I fixed the date as about 225 A.D. Twenty-two years of further study would make me modify this slightly, and fix the date as 225-50 A.D. So marked an outburst of pagan ritual, expressed in so many long inscriptions at that period, must without doubt belong to the pagan revival which marked the last struggles of the dying religion of ARTEMIS and her company against the new faith of Christianity. Memorials of that revival have been discovered during our more recent explorations; and the set of Tekmoreian documents must be added to the list. That being so, the purpose of the Tekmor becomes plain: it was in some sort of paganism and a pledge of loyalty to the Empire. The Tekmor must be ranked along with the mark on the forehead or the right hand of every worshipper of the monster in Revelation xiii. 16 (as interpreted in my "Letters to the Seven Churches," p. 111) , and along with the certificates of paganism and loyalty by which people guarded themselves against suspicion and arrest in the Decian persecution A.D. 251.

Further, the Tekmoreian inscriptions belong to the Imperial estates near Antioch. Some of the villages to which the Guest-friends belonged can be recognized as belonging to those or to other Imperial estates in Asia; it will hereafter be a subject of investigation whether all the villages may not be regarded as situated on such estates. Thus we are already able to see the high probability, nay, the practical certainty, that those great Imperial estates in Asia were the strongholds of paganism in its last struggles. This is proved independently by the well-known fact that those estates were inhabited by a far less educated and Hellenized population, and organized after a far more primitive and oriental fashion than the cities, whereas the cities were centres of education and of Christianity.

The historical results here briefly indicated would alone be a rich reward for a season's exploration; they are wide-reaching, and they throw a fresh and unexpected light on that singularly important and interesting period of the conflicts between the Imperial Government with the pagan populace and the adherents of the new faith. Yet they spring from two days' exploration at the very beginning of our work. Never before have I been so impressed with the wealth of antiquarian remains in the country. The traveller may always be certain that, wherever he is, there are plenty of relics of antiquity to be discovered; but the difficulty is to discover them. Experience, skill in dealing with the people, patience, good humour, and above all, time, are required. The oftener one travels the more one learns how much one missed in one's first essays at travel; and the chief reason of failure is want of time or patience. The young traveller is almost always too enthusiastic, too ambitious to cover a large extent of country, too eager for discovery, too much in a hurry. With few exceptions the best discoveries which I have made have been in places where I had stayed a considerable time before making the discovery, often in places which I had actually visited many times unsuccessfully. In the present year most of our time was spent in districts which have been carefully and frequently explored by eager discoverers; often on the great thoroughfares which have been traversed by scores of European travellers and observers. What is needed is to make one's way into the private courtyards and houses, to go where Mohammedan manners sternly forbid access. That is always difficult; but patience, time, and money will achieve anything. You have to find out in which of the many houses there is anything worth seeing; perhaps only one house in a hundred contains anything to reward exploration; the life of the explorer is made up of 90 per cent. of disappointment and 10 per cent. of discoveries. And, after all you must generally depart with the feeling that you are leaving a score of good things unseen, and that some more fortunate successor will discover them. You must learn to console yourself with the thought that one ought in fairness to leave something for one's successors.

For many years in earlier journeys the month of fasting in Ramazan was my enemy. Hungry and sleepy Turks proved ill-tempered and impossible to deal with; and exploration was always unfruitful for a whole month in every journey. But now Ramazan has changed round into the winter season, and is no longer the explorer's enemy; he rarely travels in winter, and, if he does, a fast for nine or ten hours in the short cold winter days does not make the natives so surly as a fast for fourteen or fifteen hours in the long, hot and dry summer days. At present my worst enemy is the nomadic habit. Many villages are entirely deserted at the time when I can travel; and little can be done in a large village, where every house and courtyard is closed up and barred, and where there is nobody to give information. The important Hittite city of Emir-Ghazi, which we discovered in 1904, remains still unexplored for that reason after two visits: only three Hittite inscriptions rewarded our search in the open ground; somebody in the winter season will find more in the houses.

A brief statement will give some idea of the archaeological wealth of the country. During nine consecutive days in June, 1905, we were at or close to fifteen ancient sites in the best explored and most accessible district of the country. Of these only one, viz., Konya, the ancient Iconium, was known and fixed as the site of an ancient town before 1901. All the others have been discovered by the explorers for our Asia Minor Exploration Fund in the last four years. Nine out of the fourteen were discovered by us this year during nine days, and the ancient names of five of them were assigned with certainty. During those nine days we also found and copied nearly 200 inscriptions, and made a number of photographs and drawings of monuments, geographical observations, etc. The published maps are extremely inaccurate, but it seems impossible in England to find any draftsman who will depart from the published maps; whatever you give him in the way of material, however carefully you draw a plan of the country which you have traversed, he finally prints only a copy from Kiepert, with the new names which you have discovered adapted, more or less badly, to the accepted misrepresentations of the country.

Perhaps the most interesting among these newly discovered towns was the ancient Zizima or Zizimma, which is still called Sizma. It lies among the hills about twelve miles north of Iconium. The quicksilver mines of this part of the country are still worked, and have been worked from time immemorial. The goddess of Zizimma, the Mother ZIZIMMENE, was the great goddess worshipped in the country round Iconium and far to the north. She was clearly indicated at Zizimma to the reverence of mankind by the subterranean wealth which she there offered for their use, and which they obtained by following the rules of mining and smelting which she herself had taught to her people. Like almost all mines in the Roman world, those at Zizimma were an Imperial estate, as is proved by an inscription which we found. We could only remain a few hours one morning at Sizma; and there is much to discover, when any explorer has time. We heard of many things there and at Nevini, a village two hours further north; but want of time, the bane of exploration, drove us onwards to a different field. Moreover, our equipment was unsuited for travel in this hilly region, and we left the Sizma district for travellers on horseback. Toward the middle of June we had the good fortune to find a group of five inscriptions in the Phrygian language, three of which are complete and certain in text. I have for twenty-five years been searching for good specimens of this kind; and this discovery will give much satisfaction to the Comparative Philolgists. One of them contains the word Bekos, which meant "bread," as we learn from HERODOTUS ii. 2, who tells of the way in which PSAMMETICHUS, King of Egypt, discovered that Phrygian was the original and natural language of mankind. He shut up two infant children along with some goats, and no man was allowed to utter a word in their hearing. At the age of two, they were found to say "Bekos," stretching forth their hands to any man who came to them — a clear proof that they were speaking Phrygian. The word was hitherto known only from the anecdote related by HERODOTUS: and it is now at last discovered in a Phrygian inscription.

The remarkable series of early Christian reliefs and inscriptions of Lycaonia, which we found in previous years, was largely increased in 1905. The symbol of a bird with a leaf in its mouth occurs on one of them, the tombstone of a Christian virgin of the later third century. The position of Lycaonia as thoroughly a Christian country already in the third century is gradually emerging before our eyes in this delightful series of inscriptions; and our knowledge of the history of Christian social development as a practical fact in the Roman empire is being pushed further and further back.

An invitation to give an address at the conclusion of the session of the American College at Scutari brought me to Constantinople in June. The kindness and hospitality shown me for twenty-four years by the American missionaries made it a duty to comply with the request. Needless to add, the duty was also a great pleasure. I had, incidentally, the long-desired opportunity of seeing a little of the Bosphorus and Sea of Marmora — for in five previous passages through Constantinople there had been no opportunity of doing so — and want of knowledge of these coasts has hitherto blocked many historical investigations. I had thought of returning to spend July in Phrygia, but decided that it was better to come home and publish at once some of our most interesting discoveries, in the hope that these might bring about further exploration in 1906; and double college work during the coming winter compels me either to use this autumn for their publication or to postpone it for a whole year. I had thought 1905 must be my last exploration for some years, because it grows more difficult to find time for travel, and college duties are likely in future to extend into the summer. But after all it seems clear that I must attempt one more exploration in 1906. As for the difficulties with which the travelling archaeologist has to contend — poor accommodation with its attendant pests, scanty food, malarial fever, and worst of all, sleeplessness — for "silent night" in or near a Turkish town or village is unknown — these are soon forgotten when they are past; and the thought of the work that still remains to be done and of the discoveries still to be made urges one to further efforts.

BIBLIOGRAPHY[1]

BOOKS BY RAMSAY

RAMSAY, SIR WILLIAM MITCHELL. *Asianic Elements in Greek Civilization.* (The Gifford Lectures in the University of Edinburgh, 1915-1916.) London: John Murray, 1927. xi, 303 pp.

——. *The Bearing of Recent Discovery on the Trustworthiness of the New Testament.* (The James Sprunt Lectures at Union Seminary, Virginia, for 1913.) London: Hodder and Stroughton, 1915. Repr. Grand Rapids, Mich.: Baker Book House, 1953. xiv, 427 pp.

——. *The Church in the Roman Empire before A.D. 170.* (Mansfield College Lectures, 1892.) 5th ed. London: Hodder and Stoughton, 1897. xxiii, 510 pp.

——. *The Cities and Bishoprics of Phrygia.* Oxford: Clarendon Press, 1895 and 1897. Vol. 1, pt. 1, xxii, 352 pp. Vol. 1, pt. 2, 353-791 pp.

——. *The Cities of St. Paul: Their Influence on His Life and Thought.* London: Hodder and Stoughton, 1907. Repr. Grand Rapids, Mich.: Baker Book House, 1960. xvi, 452 pp.

——. *The Education of Christ: Hill-Side Reveries.* London: Hodder and Stoughton, 1902. ix, 159 pp.

——. *The First Christian Century: Notes on Dr. Moffatt's Introduction to the Literature of the New Testament.* London: Hodder and Stoughton, 1911. viii, 195 pp.

——. *A Historical Commentary on St. Paul's Epistles to the Galatians.* London: Hodder and Stoughton, 1899. Repr. Grand Rapids, Mich.: Baker Book House, 1965. xi, 478 pp.

---

1 For an almost complete bibliography of all of Ramsay's writings up to 1923, see *Anatolian Studies Presented to Sir William Mitchell Ramsay,* edited by W. H. Buckler and W. M. Calder (Manchester: Manchester University Press, 1923).

——. *The Historical Geography of Asia Minor.* (Royal Geographical Society, Supplementary Paper, Vol. IV.) London: John Murray, 1890. Repr. Amsterdam: Adolph M. Hakkert, 1962. 495 pp.

——. *The Imperial Peace: An Ideal in European History.* Oxford: Clarendon Press, 1913. 28 pp.

——. *Impressions of Turkey during Twelve Years' Wanderings.* London: Hodder and Stoughton, 1897. xvi, 296 pp.

——. *The Letters to the Seven Churches of Asia and Their Place in the Plan of the Apocalypse.* London: Hodder and Stoughton, 1904. Repr. Grand Rapids, Mich.: Baker Book House, 1963. xx, 446 pp.

——. *Luke the Physician and Other Studies in the History of Religion.* London: Hodder and Stoughton, 1908. Repr. Grand Rapids, Mich.: Baker Book House, 1956. xiv, 418 pp.

——. *The Making of a University: What We Have to Learn from Educational Ideals in America.* (An Estimate of the Educational Work of Dr. Isaac Conrad Ketler.) London: Hodder and Stoughton, 1915. 46 pp.

——. *Pauline and Other Studies in Early Christian History.* London: Hodder and Stoughton, 1906. xi, 415 pp.

——. *Pictures of the Apostolic Church: Studies in the Book of Acts.* London: Hodder and Stoughton, 1910. Repr. Grand Rapids, Mich.: Baker Book House, 1959. xv 367 pp.

——. *The Revolution in Constantinople and Turkey: A Diary.* London: Hodder and Stoughton, 1909. xv, 323 pp.

——. *St. Paul the Traveller and the Roman Citizen.* London: Hodder and Stoughton, 1897. Repr. Grand Rapids, Mich.: Baker Book House, 1960. xxvii, 402 pp.

——. *St. Paul the Traveller and the Roman Citizen.* 15th ed. London: Hodder and Stoughton, 1925. xl, 402 pp.

——. *The Social Basis of Roman Power in Asia Minor.* Prepared for the press by J. G. C. Anderson. Aberdeen: Aberdeen University Press, 1941. xii, 305 pp.

——. *The Teaching of Paul in Terms of the Present Day.* London: Hodder and Stoughton, 1913. xiii, 457 pp.

——. and Miss Gertrude L. Bell. *The Thousand and One Churches.* London: Hodder and Stoughton, 1909. xiv, 580 pp.

——. *Was Christ Born at Bethlehem? A Study on the Credibility of St. Luke.* London: Hodder and Stoughton, 1898. xii, 280 pp.

ARTICLES BY RAMSAY

RAMSAY, SIR WILLIAM MITCHELL. "Achaia," *HDB*. 1:23.

——. "Adramyttium," *HDB*. 1:43.

——. "Antioch in Pisidia," *HDB*. 1:104.

——. "Asia," *HDB*. 1:171-172

——. "Asiarch," *HDB*. 1:172.

——. "Bithynia," *HDB*. 1:303.

——. "Cappadocia," *HDB*. 1:352.

——. "Caria," *HDB*. 1:354.

——. "The Census of Quirinius," *The Sunday School Times*. 64 (1922) : 764-765, 776-777.

——. "Chios," *HDB*. 1:383.

——. "Churches (Robbers of)," *HDB*. 1:441.

——. "Cilicia," *HDB*. 1:442.

——. "Cnidus," *HDB*. 1:451.

——. "Colonia Caesarea (Pisidian Antioch) in the Augustan Age," *Journal of Roman Studies*. 6 (1916) : 83-134.

——. "Colossae," *HDB*. 1:454.

——. "Corinth," *HDB*. 1:479-483.

——. "Cos," *HDB*. 1:500-501.

——. "The Cross of Christ the Center of History," *The Christian Worker's Magazine*. 14 (Nov. 1913) : 140-143. Repr. in Smith, Wilbur M. *Great Sermons on the Death of Christ*. Natick, Mass.: W. A. Wilde Co., 1965, pp. 235-241.

——. "Cutting Luke's Shipwreck Story to Pieces," *The Sunday School Times*. 28 (1916) : 355.

——. "The Date of the Apocalypse," *The Expository Times*. 16 (1905) : 171-174.

——. "Delos," *HDB*. 1:588.

——. "Derbe," *HDB*. 1:595.

——. "Diana of the Ephesians," *HDB*. 1:605-606.

——. "Ephesian," *HDB*. 1:713-714.

——. "Ephesus," *HDB*. 1:720-725.

——. "Excavating the Synagogue Church at Pisidian Antioch," *The Sunday School Times*. 73 (1931) : 575-576.

——. "Exploration of Asia Minor, as Bearing on the Historical Trustworthiness of the New Testament," *The Victoria Institute's Transactions*. 1907. pp. 201-217.

——. "Galatia," *HDB*. 2:81-89.

——. "Galatia," *The International Standard Bible Encyclopaedia*. Edited by James Orr *et al*. Grand Rapids, Mich.: William B. Eerdmans, 1939, 2:1154-1155. (Originally published in 1915.)

——. "Galatia (Region of)," *HDB*. 2:89-91.

——. "Galatians," *HDB*. 2:91-93.

——. "The Geographical Conditions Determining History and Religion in Asia Minor," *The Geographical Journal*. 20 (July-Dec. 1902) : 257-275.

——. "Halicarnassus," *HDB*. 2:286-287.

——. "Hierapolis," *HDB*. 2:379-380.

——. "A Historical Commentary on the Epistles to the Corinthians," *The Expositor*. Sixth Series, 1 (1900) : 19-31, 91-111, 203-217, 273-289, 380-387; 2 (1900) : 287-302, 368-381, 429-444; 3 (1901) : 93-110, 220-240, 343-360.

——. "A Historical Commentary on the First Epistle to Timothy," *The Expositor*. Seventh Series, 7 (1909) : 481-494; 8 (1909) : 1-21, 167-185, 264-282, 339-357, 399-416; 9 (1910) : 172-187, 319-333, 433-440; Eighth Series, 1 (1911) : 262-273, 356-375.

——. "How the Book of Acts Routed Its Higher Critics," *The Sunday School Times*. 58 (1916) : 291-292.

——. "Iconium," *Encyclopaedia Britannica*. 11th ed., 1910. 14: 271-272.

——. "Iconium," *HDB*. 2:443-445.

——. "Illyricum," *HDB*. 2:450-451.

——. "If You Had Been Traveling with Paul," *The Sunday School Times*. 63 (1921) : 540-541.

——. "The Image of the Beast in the New Testament," *The Sunday School Times*. 65 (1923) : 507.

——. "The Jews and the Graeco-Asiatic Cities," *The Expositor*. Sixth Series, 5 (1902) : 19-33, 92-109.

——. "Laodicea," *HDB*. 3:44-45.

——. "Lasea," *HDB*. 3:46.

——. "Luke's Narrative of the Birth of Christ," *The Expositor*. Eighth Series, 4 (1912) : 385-407, 481-507.

——. "Lycaonia," *Encyclopaedia Britannica*. 11th ed., 1910. 18: 151.

——. "Lycaonia," *HDB*. 3:174-175.

——. "Lycia," *HDB*. 3:176.

——. "Lydia (Place)," *HDB*. 3:177-178.

——. "Lystra," *HDB*. 3:178-180.

——. "Mallus," *HDB*. 3:223-224.

——. "Method of Research in History," *Contemporary Review*. 27 (1912) : 337-347.

——. "Miletus," *HDB*. 3:368-369.

——. "Myndus," *HDB*. 3:463-464.

——. "Myra," *HDB*. 3:464.

——. "A New Theory as to the Date of the Epistle to the Galatians," *The Expository Times*. 12 (1901) : 157-160.

——. "Nicopolis," *HDB*. 3:548-549.

——. "Numbers, Hours, Years, and Dates," *HDB*. 5:473-484.

——. "Pamphylia," *HDB*. 3:658-659.

——. "The Pastoral Epistles and Tacitus," *The Expositor*. Fourth Series, 8 (1893) : 110-119.

——. "Patara," *HDB*. 3:692.

——. "Perga," *HDB*. 3.747-749.

——. "Pergamus, Pergamum," *HDB*. 3:749-752.

——. "Phaselis," *HDB*. 3:829.

——. "Philadelphia," *HDB*. 3:830-832.

——. "Phoenix," *HDB*. 3:862-863.

——. "Phrygia," *HDB*. 3:863-869.

——. "Phrygians," *Encyclopaedia of Religion and Ethics*. Edited by James Hastings. Edinburgh: T. and T. Clark, 1917. 9:900-911.

——. "Pisidia," *HDB*. 3:884-885.

——. "Pisidian Antioch in Paul's Day and Today," *The Sunday School Times*. 67 (1925) : 415.

——. "Pontus," *HDB*. 4:15-18.

——. "Preliminary Report to the Wilson Trustees on Exploration in Phrygia and Lycaonia," *Studies in the History and Art of the Eastern Provinces of the Roman Empire*. Edited by W. M. Ramsay. (Written for the Quatercentenary of the University of Aberdeen by Seven of Its Graduates.) Aberdeen: Aberdeen University Press, 1906, pp. 231-277.

——. "Religion of Greece and Asia Minor," *HDB*. 5:109-156.

——. "Rhegium," *HDB*. 4:267-268.

——. "Rhodes," *HDB*. 4:268-269.

——. Roads and Travel in the New Testament," *HDB*. 5:375-402.

——. "Rome's Treatment of State Offenders," *The Sunday School Times*. 63 (1921) : 597-598.

——. "St. Paul at Ephesus," *The Expositor*. Fourth Series, 2 (1890) : 1-22.

——. "St. Paul's First Journey to Asia Minor," *The Expositor*. Fourth Series, 5 (1892) : 29-39.

——. "Samothrace," *HDB*. 4:377.

——. "Sardis," *HDB*. 4:404-405.

——. "A Sketch of the Geographical History of Asia Minor," *The National Geographic Magazine*. 42 (Nov. 1922) : 553-570.

——. "Sketches in the Religious Antiquities of Asia Minor," *The Annual of the British School at Athens*. 18 (1911-1912) : 37-79.

——. "Smyrna," *Encyclopaedia Britannica*. 11th ed., 1910. 25:281-282.

——. "Smyrna," *HDB*. 4:553-556.

——. "Studies in the Roman Province Galatia," *Journal of Roman Studies*. 7 (1917) :229-288, 8 (1918) : 107-145.

——. "A Summer Journey in Asia Minor," *The British Weekly*. July 27, 1905, pp. 377-378.

——. "Tarsus," *Encyclopaedia Britannica*. 11th ed., 1910. 26:433-434.

——. "Tarsus," *HDB*. 4:685.

——. "The Tekmoreian Guest-Friends: An Anti-Christian Society on the Imperial Estates at Pisidian Antioch," *Studies in the History and Art of the Eastern Provinces of the Roman Empire*. Aberdeen: Aberdeen University Press, 1906, pp. 305-377.

——. "Thracia," *HDB*. 4:754.

——. "Thyatira," *HDB*. 4:757-759.

——. "Town Clerk," *HDB*. 4:800-801.

——. "Troas," *HDB*. 4:813-814.

——. "Tyrannus," *HDB*. 4:821-823.

——. "The War of Moslem and Christian for the Possession of Asia Minor," *Studies in the History and Art of the Eastern Provinces of the Roman Empire*. Edited by W. M. Ramsay. Aberdeen: Aberdeen University Press, 1906, pp. 281-301.

——. "What Did Paul's Roman Citizenship Mean?" *The Sunday School Times*. 58 (1916) : 547, 549.

——. "Where Time Has No Value," *The Sunday School Times*. 57 (1915) : 525.

——. "When Quirinius Was Governor of Syria," *The Sunday School Times*. 64 (1922) : 559, 564.

——. "The White Stone and the 'Gladiatorial' Tessera," *The Expository Times*. 16 (1905) : 558-561.

——. "The Words in Acts Denoting Missionary Travel," *The Expositor*. Fifth Series, 1 (1895) : 385-399.

INDEX

academic honors and distinctions, 14, 17
Achaia, 32, 46
Acts, Book of, 23ff, 38ff., 61, 64
Ak-Sheher, 80
American College at Scutari, 84
Anatolia, 20
Anatolian and pre-Hellenic religion, 21
Anatolian studies, 15
Anderson, G. C., 22
Antioch, 81
Antiochus IV, 43
Apameia, 21
Apollos, 40
apologist, 38
Apostle John, 51ff.
Areopagus, 42
Artemis, 81
articles, 18, 60
> *Encyclopedia Brittanica*, 18
> *Hastings Dictionary of the Bible*, 21
> *Journal of Hellenic Studies*, 21, 80
"A Sketch of Geographic History of Asia Minor", 22
Asklepios, 54
Athena, 54
Athens, 41, 42

Barbarossa, 79
Barnabas, 24, 34, 40

Baur, Ferdinand Christian, 23, 59, 62
Bearing of Recent Discovery on the Trustworthiness of the New Testament, The, 24, 26
Bekos, 84
Bell, Gertrude, 16, 22
Benfey, Theodor, 14
Beroea, 41
Bidder, Henry Jardine, 15
birth, 13
Blaiklock, E. M. 34
Bosphorus, 85
Bruce, F. F., 26, 34, 63
Burton, E. D., 34
Byzantine Empire, 79
Byzantine roads, 20

Caesar Augustus, 35
Caesarea, 59
Cappadocia, 15
Catholic Epistles, 50, 51
census, 35, 36
Church in the Roman Empire before A.D. 170, 27f., 31
Cities and Bishoprics of Phrygia, The, 20f., 29
Cities of St. Paul, 41
Clement of Rome, 51
Colossae, 21
Colossians, Epistle to, 50, 52
Constantine, 79

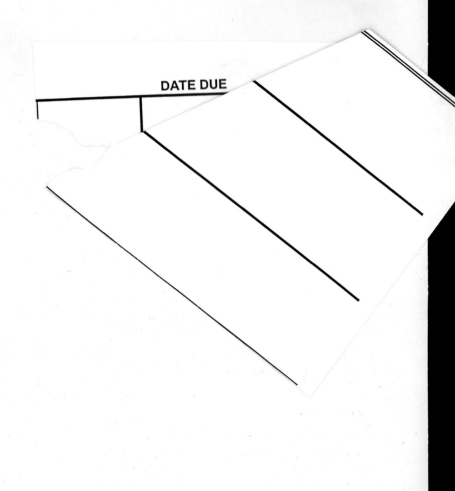

DATE DUE